The ESSEN...

EUROPEAN HISTORY

1914 to 1935
World War I and Europe in Crisis

David Crowe, Ph.D.
Professor of History
Elon College
Elon College, North Carolina

Research and Education Association
61 Ethel Road West
Piscataway, New Jersey 08854

THE ESSENTIALS ®
OF EUROPEAN HISTORY
1914 to 1935
World War I and Europe in Crisis

REVISED PRINTING, 1992

Printed in the United States of America

Library of Congress Catalog Card Number 89-62460

International Standard Book Number 0-87891-710-1

ESSENTIALS is a registered trademark of
Research and Education Association, Piscataway, New Jersey 08854

What the "Essentials of History" Will Do for You

REA's "Essentials of History" series offers a new approach to the study of history that is different from what has been available previously. Each book in the series has been designed to steer a sensible middle course, by including neither too much nor too little information.

Compared with conventional history outlines, the "Essentials of History" offer far more detail, with fuller explanations and interpretations of historical events and developments. Compared with voluminous historical tomes and textbooks, the "Essentials of History" offer a far more concise, less ponderous overview of each of the periods they cover.

The "Essentials of History" are intended primarily to aid students in studying history, doing homework, writing papers and preparing for exams. The books are organized to provide quick access to information and explanations of the important events, dates, and persons of the period. The books can be used in conjunction with any text. They will save hours of study and preparation time while providing a firm grasp and insightful understanding of the subject matter.

Instructors too will find the "Essentials of History" useful. The books can assist in reviewing or modifying course outlines. They also can assist with preparation of exams, as well as serve as an efficient memory refresher.

In sum, the "Essentials of History" will prove to be handy reference sources at all times.

The authors of the series are respected experts in their fields. They present clear, well-reasoned explanations and interpretations of the complex political, social, cultural, economic and philosophical issues and developments which characterize each era.

In preparing these books REA has made every effort to assure their accuracy and maximum usefulness. We are confident that each book will prove enjoyable and valuable to its user.

Dr. Max Fogiel, Program Director

About the Author

David Crowe is a professor at Elon College in Elon College, North Carolina, where he teaches Russian/Soviet and East Asian History. He is also chairman of the History Department and directs the college's Studies Abroad program in the USSR and Eastern Europe. Prior to coming to Elon College in 1977, he served as an archivist with National Archives of the United States and with the Department of the Army's Southeast Asian Archives. He has previously taught at the University of Georgia and DeKalb College.

Dr. Crowe has published or contributed to numerous books, including his forthcoming *The Gypsies of Eastern Europe* and *The Great Powers and the Baltic States, 1938-1940*. He has published numerous articles on minorities in Eastern Europe and the Soviet Union, Soviet and Chinese foreign policy, the Holocaust, and other topics in scholarly journals and encyclopedias. He serves on the Editorial Board of Nationalities Papers, is a Vice Chairman of the Association for the Study of Nationalities (USSR and East Europe), and has been a Reader for the Department of Education's Fulbright grants for doctoral and post-doctoral proposals in Eastern Europe and the Soviet Union.

CONTENTS

Chapter No.		Page No.
1	**THE ORIGINS OF WORLD WAR I**	**1**
1.1	Historical Background	1
1.1.1	Balance of Power and Europe's Alliance System	2
1.1.2	Arms Buildup and Imperialism	2
1.2	Immediate Cause of World War I	3
1.2.1	The Balkan Crisis	3
1.3	The Outbreak of the World War	3
1.3.1	Assassination and Reprisals	3
1.3.2	The Conflict Expands	5
1.3.3	Germany and the Schlieffen Plan	5
1.3.4	War Begins	5
1.4	The War in 1914	6
1.4.1	The Western Front	6
1.4.2	The Eastern Front	6
1.5	The War in 1915	8
1.5.1	The Western Front	8
1.5.2	The Eastern Front	9
1.5.3	The Eastern Mediterranean	10

1.5.4	The Middle East, 1914 – 1916	10
1.6	The War in 1916	11
1.6.1	The Western Front	11
1.6.2	The Eastern Front	11
1.6.3	Central Powers Propose Peace Talks	12
1.6.4	War on the High Seas, 1914 – 1916	12
1.6.5	New Military Technology	13
2	**THE RUSSIAN REVOLUTIONS OF 1917**	**16**
2.1	Historical Background	16
2.1.1	The Russo-Japanese War and the 1905 Revolution	17
2.1.2	Era of Reaction and Reforms, 1906 – 1912	17
2.1.3	Rasputin and Upheaval, 1912 – 1914	18
2.2	Russia at War: The Home Front, 1914 – 1917	18
2.2.1	The Military	18
2.2.2	The Civilian Economy	18
2.2.3	The Government and the Bureaucracy	19
2.3	The February Revolution	19
2.3.1	Riots and Strikes	19
2.3.2	The Duma	20
2.4	The Provisional Government in Power (March – November 1917)	20
2.4.1	Leadership	20
2.4.2	Problems	21
2.5	The Petrograd Soviet	21
2.5.1	Creation	21

2.5.2	Policies	22
2.6	Lenin Returns to Russia	22
2.6.1	The April Theses	22
2.7	The First Coalition	23
2.8	The July Crises	23
2.8.1	The July Offensive	24
2.8.2	The Second Coalition	24
2.8.3	The July Days	24
2.9	The Second Coalition and the Kornilov Affair	25
2.9.1	The Moscow State Conference (August 26 – 28)	25
2.9.2	The Kornilov Affair	26
2.9.3	The Third Coalition	26
2.10	The Bolshevik October Revolution	26
2.10.1	Lenin's Decision to Seize Power	27
2.10.2	Trotsky and the Military Revolutionary Committee	27
2.10.3	The Coup of November 6 – 7	27
2.10.4	The II Congress of Soviets	27
2.11	The Constituent Assembly	28
3	**WORLD WAR I: THE FINAL PHASE, 1917 – 1918**	**30**
3.1	The Western Front, 1917	30
3.1.1	The French Offensive	30
3.1.2	The British Offensive	31
3.1.3	The Italian Front and the Battle of Caporetto	31

3.1.4   The Tank Battle of Cambrai   31

3.2   The Middle and Near East, 1917   32

3.2.1   Mesopotamia   32

3.2.2   Palestine   32

3.3   The U.S. Enters The War   32

3.3.1   American Neutrality   32

3.3.2   The U.S. and Freedom of the Seas   32

3.3.3   Germany and Submarine Warfare   33

3.3.4   The Zimmerman Telegram   33

3.4   Russia Leaves the War   33

3.4.1   The Armistice at Brest-Litovsk   34

3.4.2   Trotsky and Initial Peace Negotiations
        with Germany   34

3.4.3   Soviet Differences Over Peace Terms   34

3.4.4   Negotiations Resume at Brest-Litovsk   35

3.4.5   The Soviet Response and the Treaty of
        Brest-Litovsk   35

3.5   The Allied Breakthrough   35

3.5.1   The American Presence: Naval and
        Economic Support   36

3.5.2   The German Offensive of 1918   36

3.5.3   The Allied Offensive of 1918   37

3.6   The Armistice with Germany   38

3.7   The Collapse of the German Monarchy and
        the Creation of the German Republic   38

4	**THE PARIS PEACE CONFERENCE OF 1919 – 1920**	**39**
4.1	War Losses and Their Impact on the Peace Conference	39
4.2	Woodrow Wilson and the Fourteen Points	40
4.3	Secret Allied Agreements Concluded During World War I	41
4.4	Preliminary Discussions	42
4.4.1	France and the Rhineland Conflict	43
4.4.2	German Disarmament	43
4.4.3	Reparations	43
4.5	The Treaty of Versailles	43
4.5.1	Most Significant Clauses	44
4.5.2	German Hesitance to Sign the Treaty	45
4.6	Treaties with Germany's Allies	46
4.6.1	The Treaty of St. Germain (September 10, 1919)	46
4.6.2	Treaty of Neuilly (November 27, 1919)	46
4.6.3	Treaty of Trianon (June 4, 1920)	46
4.6.4	Treaty of Sevres (August 10, 1920)	46
4.7	Problems of Allied Unity: Japan, Italy, and the U.S.	47
4.7.1	Japan	47
4.7.2	Italy	47
4.7.3	The United States	48
5	**POLITICAL DEVELOPMENTS IN POST-WAR EUROPE, 1918 – 1929**	**50**
5.1	England	50
5.1.1	England, 1918 – 1922	50

5.1.2	Politics, 1922 – 1924	51
5.1.3	England and Stanley Baldwin, 1924 – 1929	52
5.2	France	52
5.2.1	The Bloc National, 1919 – 1924	53
5.2.2	The Cartel des Gauches, 1924 – 1926	54
5.2.3	The Union Nationale, 1926 – 1928	54
5.3	Weimar Germany, 1918 – 1929	55
5.3.1	Provisional Government	55
5.3.2	Problems of the Weimar Republic, 1919 – 1920	57
5.3.3	Weimar Politics, 1919 – 1923	58
5.3.4	The Policies of Gustav Stresemann	59
5.3.5	Weimar Politics, 1924 – 1928	60
5.4	Italy	61
5.4.1	Italian Politics, 1918 – 1919	61
5.4.2	Government of Giovanni Giolitti, 1920 – 1921	61
5.4.3	Benito Mussolini and Italian Fascism	62
5.4.4	Mussolini's Consolidation of Power	63
5.4.5	Consolidation of the Dictatorship	64
5.4.6	The Fascist Party	65
5.4.7	The Syndicalist-Corporate System	65
5.4.8	Foreign Policy	66
5.5	Soviet Russia	67
5.5.1	Origins of the Russian Civil War, 1918	67
5.5.2	The Russian Civil War, 1919 – 1920	68
5.5.3	Domestic Policy and Upheaval, 1918 – 1921	69
5.5.4	The New Economic Policy, 1921 – 1927	70
5.5.5	The Death of Lenin and the Rise of Josef Stalin	70

5.5.6	The Struggle for Power, 1924 – 1925	71
5.5.7	The Struggle for Power, 1925 – 1927	72
5.5.8	Soviet Constitutional Development	73
5.5.9	Foreign Policy, 1918 – 1929	74

6	**EUROPE IN CRISIS: DEPRESSION AND DICTATORSHIP, 1929 – 1935**	**76**
6.1	England	76
6.1.1	Ramsay MacDonald and the Depression, 1929 – 1931	76
6.1.2	The "National Government," 1931 – 1935	77
6.1.3	The Election of 1935	77
6.2	France	77
6.2.1	France Under Andre Tardieu, 1929 – 1932	77
6.2.2	Return of the Cartel des Gauches, 1932 – 1934	78
6.2.3	Struggle for Stability, 1934 – 1935	79
6.3	Germany	80
6.3.1	The Young Plan	80
6.3.2	Germany and the Depression	80
6.3.3	The Rise of Adolf Hitler and Nazism	81
6.3.4	The Nazi Movement, 1924 – 1929	82
6.3.5	Weimar Politics, 1930 – 1933	82
6.3.6	Hitler Becomes Chancellor	84
6.3.7	Hitler Consoldiates Power	85
6.3.8	Religion and Anti-Semitism	86
6.3.9	International Affairs	86
6.4	Italy	87

6.4.1	Fascist Economic Reforms	87
6.4.2	Church and State	88
6.4.3	Foreign Policy	89
6.5	Soviet Russia	92
6.5.1	Collectivization of Soviet Agriculture	92
6.5.2	Industrialization	93
6.5.3	Party Politics and the Origin of the Purges	94
6.5.4	Foreign Policy, 1929 – 1935	95

7	**INTERNATIONAL DEVELOPMENTS, 1918 – 1935**	**96**
7.1	The League of Nations	96
7.1.1	The Preamble of the League's Covenant	97
7.1.2	The Organization of the League of Nations	97
7.2	The Washington Conference, 1921 – 1922	99
7.2.1	The Washington Naval Treaty (Five Power Treaty)	99
7.2.2	The Four Power Treaty	99
7.2.3	The Nine Power Treaty	99
7.3	The Draft Treaty of Mutual Assistance (1923)	100
7.4	The Geneval Protocol (1924)	100
7.5	The Locarno Pact (1925)	101
7.5.1	Treaty of Mutual Guarantees (Rhineland Pact)	101
7.5.2	Arbitration Settlements	102
7.5.3	Eastern Accords	102
7.5.4	Germany Joins the League	102
7.6	The Pact of Paris (Kellogg-Briand Pact)	102

7.7	The Waning Search for Disarmament	103
7.7.1	London Naval Disarmament Treaty	103
7.7.2	World Disarmament Conference	103
7.8	League and Allied Response to Aggression	104
7.8.1	The League's Lytton Report and Manchuria	104
7.8.2	The Stresa Front	105
7.8.3	Italy and Ethiopia	105

CHAPTER 1

THE ORIGINS OF WORLD WAR I

In August 1914, most of the world's major powers became engaged in a conflict that most people welcomed romantically and felt would last only a few months. Instead, a war of world dimensions evolved that saw the clash of outdated military values with modern technological warfare. A war that most welcomed and that no one seemed to be able to win lasted over four years, and resulted in 12 million deaths.

1.1   HISTORICAL BACKGROUND

The long-range roots of the origins of World War I can be traced to numerous factors, beginning with the creation of modern Germany in 1871. Achieved through a series of wars, the emergence of this new German state completely destroyed Europe's traditional balance-of-power, and forced its diplomatic and military planners back to their drawing boards to rethink their collective strategies to maintain proper military and diplomatic balance. In the period between 1871 and 1914, a number of developments took place that intensified tensions between the major powers.

1.1.1 *Balance of Power and Europe's Alliance System*

One of the collective themes in 19th century Europe's diplomatic arena was an effort by the major powers to organize their international relationships in such a way to keep any single or collective group of nations from gaining a dominant diplomatic or military advantage on the Continent.

From 1871 to 1890, this balance was maintained through the network of alliances created by the German Chancellor, Otto von Bismarck, and centered around his *Dreikaiserbund* (League of the Three Emperors) that isolated France, and the Dual (Germany, Austria) and Triple (Germany, Austria, Italy) Alliances. Bismarck's fall in 1890 resulted in new policies that saw Germany move closer to Austria, while England and France (*Entente Cordiale*, 1904), and later Russia (*Triple Entente*, 1907), drew closer.

1.1.2 *Arms Buildup and Imperialism*

Germany's dramatic defeat of France in 1870 – 71 with one of Europe's most up-to-date armies, coupled with Kaiser Wilhelm II's decision in 1890 to build up a navy comparable to that of Great Britain created a reactive arms race that haunted Europe. This, blended with European efforts to carve out colonial empires in Africa and Asia – plus a new spirit of nationalism and the growing romanticization of war – helped create an unstable international environment in the years before the outbreak of the World War.

1.2   IMMEDIATE CAUSE OF WORLD WAR I

1.2.1   *The Balkan Crisis*

The Balkans, that area of Europe that now comprises Yugoslavia, Albania, Greece, Bulgaria, and Rumania, was Europe's most unstable area. Part of the rapidly decaying Ottoman (Turkish) Empire, it saw two forces – ethnic nationalism among the various small groups that lived there, and competition between Austria-Hungary and Russia over spheres-of-influence in this region – complicate an already unstable situation. Friction was intense in the region between Austria and Serbia, particularly after the former annexed Bosnia and Herzegovina in 1908, regions desired by Serbia. In 1912, with Russian encouragement, a Balkan League of Serbia, Montenegro, Greece, and Bulgaria went to war with Turkey. Serbia, which wanted a spot on the Adriatic, was rebuffed when Austria created Albania to deter Serbia. This intensified bitterness between both countries, and prompted Russia to take a more protective attitude toward its Southern Slavic cousins.

1.3   THE OUTBREAK OF THE WORLD WAR

1.3.1   *Assassination and Reprisals*

On June 28, 1914, the Archduke Franz Ferdinand (1863 – 1914), heir to the Austrian throne, was assassinated by Gavrilo Princip, a young Serbian nationalist working for Serbian Army Intelligence in Sarajevo, capital of Bosnia. Austria's rulers felt the murder provided them with an opportunity to move against Serbia and end anti-Austrian unrest in the Balkans. After consultation with the German government, which on July 6 gave Austria a blank check to take whatever steps necessary to punish Serbia, the Austrian government presented Serbia with eleven threatening demands on July 23, 1914. They required Serbia to suppress and punish all forms of anti-Austrian senti-

3

THE BALKANS, 1912-1914

RUMANIA

BOSNIA

(from Bulgaria)

(Area acquired from Turkey)

SERBIA

BULGARIA

BLACK SEA

MONTENEGRO

ALBANIA

(Area acquired from Turkey)

(Area acquired from Turkey)

(Area acquired from Turkey)

GREECE

TURKEY

DODECANESE
(It. Occupation)

MEDITERRANEAN SEA

CRETE
(Gr., Acq. from Turkey)

ment there with the help of Austrian officials. On July 25, 1914, three hours after mobilizing its army, Serbia accepted most of Austria's terms with qualifications.

1.3.2 The Conflict Expands

Austria immediately broke official relations with Serbia and mobilized its army, while between July 18 – 24, Russia let the Austrians and the Germans know that it intended fully to back Serbia in the dispute. France, Russia's ally, voiced support of Russia's moves. On July 28, 1914, Austria went to war against Serbia, and began to bombard Belgrade the following day. At the same time, Russia gradually prepared for war against Austria and Germany, declaring full mobilization on July 30.

1.3.3 Germany and the Schlieffen Plan

German military strategy, based in part on the plan of the Chief of the General Staff from 1891 to 1905, Count Alfred von Schlieffen, viewed Russian mobilization as an act of war. Based on a two front war with Russia and France, it was predicated on a swift, decisive blow against France while maintaining a defensive position against slowly mobilizing Russia, which would be dealt with after France. It required an attack in France through neutral Belgium which would bring England into the war as a protector of Belgian neutrality.

1.3.4 War Begins

Germany demanded that Russia demobilize in 12 hours, and appealed to its ambassador in Berlin. Russia's offer to negotiate the matter was rejected, and Germany declared war on Russia on August 1, 1914. Germany asked France its intentions and Paris replied that it would respond according to its own interests. On August 3, Germany declared war on France.

EUROPEAN POWERS' PLANS FOR WAR, 1914

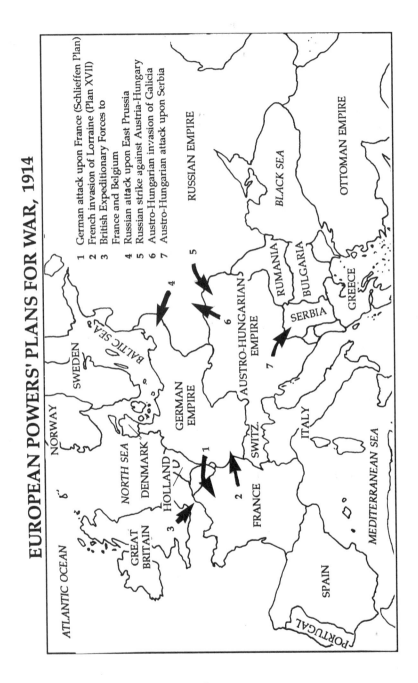

1 German attack upon France (Schlieffen Plan)
2 French invasion of Lorraine (Plan XVII)
3 British Expeditionary Forces to France and Belgium
4 Russian attack upon East Prussia
5 Russian strike against Austria-Hungary
6 Austro-Hungarian invasion of Galicia
7 Austro-Hungarian attack upon Serbia

Berlin asked Belgium for permission to send its troops through its territory to attack France, which Belgium refused. On August 4, England, which had agreed in 1839 to protect Belgian neutrality, declared war on Germany; Belgium followed suit. Between 1914 and 1915, the alliance of the *Central Powers* (Germany, Austria-Hungary, Bulgaria, and Turkey) faced the *Allied Powers* of England, France, Russia, Japan, and in 1917, the United States. A number of smaller countries were also part of the Allied coalition.

1.4   THE WAR IN 1914

1.4.1   *The Western Front*

Germany attacks France. After entering Belgium, the Germans attacked France on five fronts in an effort to encircle Paris rapidly. France was defeated in the Battle of the Frontier (August 14 – 24) in Lorraine, the Ardennes, and in the Charleroi-Mons area. However, the unexpected Russian attack in East Prussia and Galicia from August 17 to 20 forced Germany to transfer important forces eastward to halt the Russian drive.

Battle of the Marne (September 5 – 9). To halt a further German advance, the French army, aided by Belgian and English forces, counterattacked. They stopped the German drive and forced small retreats, while mutual outflanking maneuvers created a battle front that would determine the demarcation of the Western Front for the next 4 years. It ran, in uneven fashion, from the North Sea through Belgium and northern France to Switzerland.

1.4.2   *The Eastern Front*

Early Russian Offensive. Russian forces under Pavel Rennenkampf and Aleksandr Samsonov, invaded East Prussia

7

and Galicia in mid-August. With only 9 of 87 divisions in the east, the German defense faltered. Generals Paul von Hindenburg and Erich Ludendorff, aided by two corps from the Western Front, were sent on August 23 to revive the Eighth Army in East Prussia.

Battles of Tannenberg (August 25 – 31) *and Mazurian Lakes* (September 6 – 15). The Russian 2nd Army under Samsonov met the German Eighth Army. Suffering from poor communications and Rennenkampf's refusal to send his 1st Army to aid him during most of the battle, Samsonov surrendered with 90,000 troops and committed suicide. Moving northward, the German 8th Army now confronted Rennenkampf's 1st Army. After an unsuccessful initial encounter against the Germans, Rennenkampf rapidly retreated, suffering significant losses.

Russian Successes in Galicia. Nikolai Ivanov's Southwest Army group enjoyed some successes against Austro-Hungarian forces in Galicia and southern Poland throughout August. By the end of 1914, they were poised to strike deeper into the area.

Battle for Warsaw and Lodz. The Germans retreated after their assault against Warsaw in late September, while Hindenburg's attack on Lodz ten days after he was appointed Commander-in-Chief of the Eastern Front (Nov. 1) was more successful; by the end of 1914 this important textile center was in German hands.

1.5   THE WAR IN 1915

1.5.1   *The Western Front*

With Germany concentrating on the East, France and England launched a series of small attacks throughout the year that resulted in a few gains and extremely heavy casualties. Wooed by both sides, Italy joined the Allies and declared war on the Central Powers on May 23 after signing the secret Treaty of London on April 26 which, if victorious, gave Italy Austrian provinces in the north and some Turkish territory. Italian attacks against Austria in the Isonzo area towards Trieste were unsuccessful because of difficult terrain, and failed to lessen pressure on the Russians in the East.

1.5.2 *The Eastern Front*

The Austrian-German Offensive. On January 23, 1915, Austro-German forces began a coordinated offensive in East Russia and in the Carpathians. The two-pronged German assault in the north was stopped by February 27, while Austrian efforts to relieve their besieged defensive network at Przemysl failed when it fell into Russian hands on March 22, with great Austrian losses. In early March, Russian forces under Nikolai Ivanov drove deeper into the Carpathians with inadequate materiel support.

The German Counteroffensive. To halt the Russian drive, German forces, strengthened by troops from the Western Front under August von Mackensen, began a move on May 2 to strike at the heart of the Russian Front. They used the greatest artillery concentration of the war to that time as part of their strategy. In June, Mackensen shifted his assault towards Lublin and Brest-Litovsk, while the German XII army in the north, and the X and Niemen armies, moved toward Kovno in the Baltic. By August 1915, much of Russian Poland was in German hands.

Aid to Serbia. In an effort to provide direct access to the Turks defending Gallipoli, Germany and Austria invaded Serbia in the early fall, aided by their new ally, Bulgaria. Defeated by October 7, the Serbian army retreated to Corfu. Belated

Allied efforts to ship troops from Gallipoli to help Bulgaria failed.

Command Changes. Allied frustration resulted in the appointment of Marshal Joseph Joffre as French Commander-in-Chief and Field Marshal Douglas Haig as British Commander in December 1915.

1.5.3   The Eastern Mediterranean

Turkey Enters the War. Turkey entered the war on the Central Power side on October 28, 1914, which prevented the shipment of Anglo-French aid to Russians through the Straits.

Churchill and the Dardanelles. The Western stalemate caused Allied strategists to look to the eastern Mediterranean for a way to break the military deadlock. Winston Churchill, Britain's First Lord of the Admiralty, devised a plan to seize the Straits of the Dardanelles to open lines to Russia, take Constantinople, and isolate Turkey. These efforts between February 19 and March 18, 1915, were unsuccessful.

The Gallipoli Campaign. On April 25, Allied forces invaded Gallipoli Peninsula in a different attempt to capture the Straits. Turkish troops offered strong resistance, and forced the Allies (after suffering 252,000 casualties) to begin a three week evacuation that began on December 20, 1915.

1.5.4   The Middle East, 1914 – 1916

In an effort to protect its petroleum interests in the Persian Gulf, an Anglo-Indian force took Al Basrals (Basra) in Southern Iraq in November 1915. The following year, British forces moved north and took Al Kut (Kut al Irnara) from Turkey on September 28. To counter failures on the Western Front, British forces now tried to take Baghdad, but were stopped by the

Turks at Ctesiphon on November 22. Turkish forces besieged Al Kut on December 8, and captured it on April 29, 1916. Two-thirds of the 10,000 captured British POW's died of Turkish mistreatment.

1.6 THE WAR IN 1916

1.6.1 *The Western Front*

In order to break the stalemate on the Western Front and drain French forces in the effort, the Germans decided to attack the French fortress town of Verdun.

Battle for Verdun (February 21 – December 18, 1916). From February until June, German forces, aided by closely coordinated heavy artillery barrages, assaulted the forts around Verdun. The Germans suffered 281,000 casualties while the French, under Marshal Henri Petain, lost 315,000 in successfully defending their position.

Battle of the Somme (July 1 – November 18). To take pressure off the French, an Anglo-French force mounted three attacks on the Germans to the left of Verdun in July, September and November. In the end, German pressure was reduced, but at great loss. Anglo-French casualties totaled 600,000.

1.6.2 *The Eastern Front*

Initially, the Allies had hoped for a general coordinated attack on all fronts against the Central Powers. Now efforts centered on relieving pressure at Verdun and on the Italians at Trentino.

The Brusilov Offensive (June 4 – September 20). Orchestrated by Aleksei Brusilov, it envisoned a series of unexpected attacks along a lengthy front to confuse the enemy. By late August, he had advanced into Galicia and the Carpathians. Enemy dead, wounded and captured were 1.5 million, while the Russian losses were 500,000.

Rumania Enters the War (August 27). As a result of Russian successes and the secret Treaty of Bucharest (August 17) in which Rumania would get Transylvania, Bukovina, the Banat and part of the Hungarian Plain if the Allies won, Rumania entered the war on the Allied side. The Rumanian thrust into Transylvania was pushed back, and on December 6, a German-Bulgarian army occupied Bucharest as well as the bulk of Rumania.

1.6.3 *Central Powers Propose Peace Talks*

The death of Austrian Emperor Franz Joseph on November 21 prompted his successor, Charles VIII, to discuss the prospect of peace terms with his allies. On December 12, the four Central Powers, strengthened by the fall of Bucharest, offered four separate peace proposals, based on their recent military achievements. The Allies rejected them on December 30 because they felt them insincere.

1.6.4 *War on the High Seas, 1914 – 1916*

Allied Strategy. Britain's naval strategy in the first year of the war was to disrupt totally German shipping world-wide with the aid of the French and the Japanese. Germany sought ways to defend itself and weaken Allied naval strength. By the end of 1914, Allied fleets had gained control of the high seas, which caused Germany to lose control of its colonial empire.

Submarine Warfare (1914 – 1916). Germany's failure in 1914 to weaken British naval strength prompted German naval leaders to begin to use the submarine as an offensive weapon to weaken the British. On February 4, Germany announced a war zone around the British Isles, and advised neutral powers to sail there at their own risk. Regardless, a German submarine sank a British passenger vessel, the *Lusitania*, on May 7, 1915, because it was secretly carrying arms. Attacked off of the coast of Ireland, there were 1201 casualties, including 139 Americans.

American Protests. The United States protested the sinking as a violation of the Declaration of London (1909). After four months of negotiations, Germany agreed not to sink any passenger vessels without warning, and to help all passengers and crew to life boats. Germany shifted its U-boat activity to the Mediterranean.

Battle of Jutland/Skagerrak (May 31 – June 1916). The main naval battle of World War I pitted 28 British dreadnoughts and 9 cruisers against 16 German dreadnoughts and 5 cruisers. Over 250 ships took part. In the end, the battle was a draw, with England losing 14 ships and Germany 11. It forced the German High Sea Fleet not to venture out of port for the rest of the war. Instead, they concentrated on use of the U-boat.

1.6.5 New Military Technology

Submarine. Germany, Russia, and Great Britain all had submarines, though the Germans used their U-boats most effectively. Designed principally for coastal protection, they increasingly used them to reduce British naval superiority through tactical and psychological means.

Machine Guns and Tanks. By the spring of 1915, British war planners finally awoke to the fact that the machine gun had become the mistress of defensive trench warfare. In a search for a weapon to counter trench defenses, the British developed tanks as an armored "land ship," and first used them on September 15, 1916, in the battle of the Somme. Their value was not immediately realized because there were too few of them to be effective, and interest in them waned. Renewed interest came in 1917.

Aircraft. Airplanes were initially used for observation purposes in the early months of the war. As their numbers grew, mid-air struggles using pistols and rifles took place, until the Germans devised a synchronized propeller and machine gun on its Fokker aircraft in May 1915. The Allies responded with similar equipment and new squadron tactics during the early days of the Verdun campaign in February 1916, and briefly gained control of the skies. They also began to use their aircraft for bombing raids against Zeppelin bases in Germany. Air supremacy shifted to the Germans in 1917.

During the first year of the war, the Germans began to use Zeppelin airships to bomb civilian targets in England. Though their significance was neutralized with the development of the explosive shell in 1916, Zeppelins played an important role as a psychological weapon in the first two years of the war.

Gas. In the constant search for methods to counter trench warfare, the Germans and the Allied forces experimented with various forms of internationally outlawed gas. On October 27, 1914, the Germans tried a nose/eye irritant gas at Neuve-Chapelle, and by the spring of 1915 had developed an asphyxiating lachaymatory chlorine gas at the battle of Spres. The British countered with a similar chemical at the battles of Champagne and Loos that fall. Military strategists initially had little faith in gas since its use depended heavily on wind conditions, which could change the direction of the gas at any moment. However, as they desperately struggled to find ways to break the deadlock on the Western Front, they devised tactics and protection methods that enabled them to integrate the use of gas into their strategy.

MILITARY OPERATIONS OF WORLD WAR I

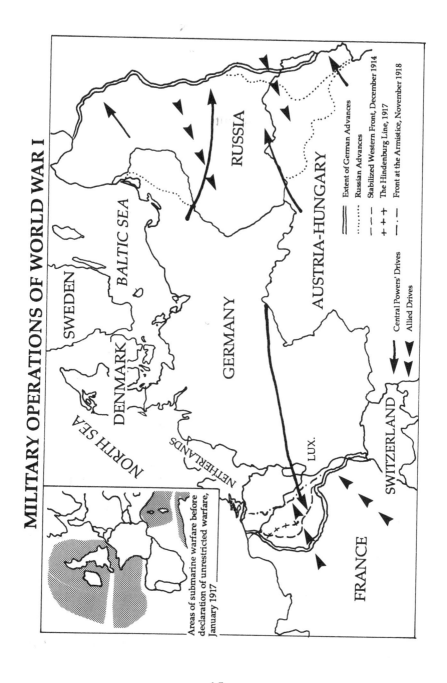

NORTH SEA

SWEDEN

BALTIC SEA

DENMARK

NETHERLANDS

GERMANY

RUSSIA

LUX.

AUSTRIA-HUNGARY

FRANCE

SWITZERLAND

Areas of submarine warfare before declaration of unrestricted warfare, January 1917

——— Extent of German Advances
·········· Russian Advances
– – – Stabilized Western Front, December 1914
+ + + The Hindenburg Line, 1917
–·– Front at the Armistice, November 1918

Central Powers' Drives
Allied Drives

CHAPTER 2

THE RUSSIAN
REVOLUTIONS OF 1917

Two events that would have a dramatic impact on the war
and the world were the February and October Revolutions in
1917. The former toppled the Romanov Dynasty and spawned
that country's brief flirtation with democracy under the temporary Provisional Government. It collapsed later that year as a
result of the October Revolution, which brought Lenin and his
Bolshevik faction to power.

2.1   HISTORICAL BACKGROUND

Plagued for centuries by a backward autocratic government
and a rural serf economy, Russia seemed on the verge of dramatic change after Tsar Alexander II (1855 – 1881) freed the
serfs in 1861. Emancipation, however, coupled with other important government and social reforms, created chaos nationwide and helped stimulate a new class of violent revolutionaries bent on destroying the Tsarist system. Terrorists murdered
Alexander II, which prompted the country's last two rulers,

Alexander III (1881 – 1894) and Nicholas II (1894 – 1917) to turn the clock backward politically.

2.1.1 *The Russo-Japanese War and the 1905 Revolution*

In February 1904, war broke out between Russia and Japan over spheres-of-influence in Korea and Manchuria. Russia's inability to support adequately its military forces in Asia, coupled with growing battlefield losses, prompted a revolution nationwide after police fired on peaceful demonstrators in January 1905. A groundswell of strikes and demonstrations swept the country and neutralized the government, which was on the verge of collapse. Nicholas II survived because he agreed in his October Manifesto (October 30, 1905) to create a constitution, share power with a legislature (Duma), and grant civil rights. This decree defused the crisis and enabled the government to survive and rebuild its political base.

2.1.2 *Era of Reaction and Reforms, 1906 – 1912*

Once the Tsar had diminished the threat to his throne, and felt more comfortable, he issued the **Fundamental Laws** (May 6, 1906), which severely limited the power of the Duma. Regardless, over the next eleven years, four growingly conservative Dumas met, and provided a tradition of constitutional governments for the country. This, blended with the emergence of workers' and soldiers' *Soviets* (councils), and political parties (**Kadets, Constitutional Democrats; Octobrists**), created an atmosphere of challenge and change for Russia. To counter this mood, the Tsar appointed Peter Stolypin as Prime Minister (1906 – 1911) to initiate mollifying reforms for the peasants and develop a private agricultural system throughout the country. These efforts, and an industrial boom, saw Russia finally begin to realize its economic potential.

17

2.1.3 *Rasputin and Upheaval, 1912 – 1914*

The death of Stolypin in 1911, coupled with a governmental system incapable of dealing with new labor unrest associated with industrial development, brought to the fore a semi-illiterate holy man, Gregorii Rasputin, who, because he seemed to possess powers to save the Tsar's hemophiliac son, Alexei, obtained tremendous influence over the royal family.

2.2 RUSSIA AT WAR: THE HOME FRONT, 1914 – 1917

Russia's entrance into the World War was met with broad public acceptance and support. Serious problems, however, plagued the government, the military, and the economy that threatened to undermine a military effort that most expected would win the war in a matter of months.

2.2.1 *The Military*

The draft increased Russia's armed forces from 1,350,000 to 6,500,000 during the war, though the government was only able to equip fully a small percentage of these troops. In addition, the country's military leaders differed on whether to concentrate their efforts on the Austrians or the Germans, while in the field, commanders were handicapped by inadequate communication and maps. As a result, German drives in the spring and summer of 1915 saw Russian spirit collapse as defensive efforts proved ineffective. However, by the end of that year, High Command personnel changes, aided by new industrial output, enabled the Russians to briefly turn the tide of battle.

2.2.2 *The Civilian Economy*

At first, Russian agricultural production proved adequate for the war's needs, but in time, because of growing labor shortages, production of foodstuffs fell by one-third, while the military only received about one-half of their grain requests because of the collapse of the transportation system. Regardless, by 1917, the country still had enough food for its military and civilian population. Skilled labor shortages, the loss of Poland, and inadequate government planning kept industry from producing the materiel necessary to supply the military. Consequently, despite a trade surplus in 1914, Russia encumbered a trade deficit of 2.5 billion rubles by 1917 from its Allies.

2.2.3 The Government and the Bureaucracy

As the country's problems mounted, the Tsar responded by assuming direct command of his army on the front in September 1915, leaving the government in the hands of his wife, Alexandra, and Rasputin. Those in government who appeared critical of the Tsar's policies were dismissed, and in time the country lost its most effective leaders. The Duma, which was forced to assume more and more leadership responsibilities, formed the Progressive Bloc, a coalition mainly of Kadets and Octobrists, in an effort to try to force the Tsar to appoint more competent officials. The Tsar's refusal to accept this group's proposals led to increasing criticism of his policies. In November 1916, distant relatives of the Tsar and a Duma member secretly murdered Rasputin.

2.3 THE FEBRUARY REVOLUTION

The February Revolution, so named because the Russian calendar at the time was 13 days behind that of the West, was a spontaneous series of events that forced the collapse of the Romanov Dynasty.

2.3.1 Riots and Strikes

Growing discontent with the government's handling of the

war saw a new wave of civilian unrest engulf the country. Estimates are that 1,140 such occurrences swept Russia in January and February, which prompted officials to send extra troops into Petrograd (old St. Petersburg) to protect the royal family. Particularly troublesome were food riots. Military and police units ordered to move against the mobs either remained at their posts or joined them.

2.3.2 *The Duma*

Though ordered by the Tsar not to meet until April, Duma leaders began to demand dramatic solutions to the country's problems. Its President, M. V. Rodzianko, was in constant consultation with the Tsar about the growing crisis. On March 12, he informed Nicholas II that civil war had broken out, and that he needed to create a new cabinet responsible to the legislature. Though dissolved on March 11, the Duma met in special session on March 13 and created a Provisional Committee of Elders to deal with the unrest. After two days of discussions, it decided that the Tsar must give up his throne, and on March 15, 1917, Rodzianko and A. I. Guchkov, leader of the Octobrist Party, convinced the Tsar to abdicate. He agreed and turned the throne over to his brother, the Grand Duke Michael, who gave it up the following day.

2.4   THE PROVISIONAL GOVERNMENT IN POWER (March – November, 1917)

From March through November 1917, a temporary Provisional Government ruled Russia. It tried to move the country towards democracy and keep Russia in the war as a loyal western ally.

2.4.1 *Leadership*

The principle figures in the new government were Prince

George Lvov, a Kadet Party and *zemstvo* leader, who served as Prime Minister and Minister of the Interior; Paul Miliukov, head of the Kadet Party, Foreign Minister; A.I. Guchkov, an Octobrist leader, Minister of War; and Alexander Kerensky, a conservative Socialist Revolutionary and Vice-Chairman of the Petrograd Soviet, Minister of Justice.

2.4.2 *Problems*

The Provisional Government was made up of middle class and intellectual leaders, and had little contact or sympathy with the problems or concerns of the workers or peasants. Its leaders, particularly Miliukov, felt the government had to remain a loyal ally and stay in the war to maintain its international credibility. Despite pressure to redistribute land, Lvov's government felt that it did not have the authority to deal with this complex issue. Instead, it left the problem to a future Constituent Assembly that would convene within a year. The Provisional Government did, however, implement a number of far-reaching reforms, including full political and religious freedom, election of local officials, an eight hour working day, and legal and judicial changes.

2.5   THE PETROGRAD SOVIET

On the eve of Nicholas II's abdication, a "shadow government," the Petrograd Soviet, was formed from among the capital's workers, and took control of the city administration. Briefly, it shared the Tauride Palace with the Provisional Government.

2.5.1 *Creation*

On March 13, delegates were elected to a Soviet of Worker's Deputies, later renamed the Soviet of Workers and

Soldiers Deputies. It was made up of 1,300 representatives, and grew to 3,000 the following week with the addition of military delegates. Because of its size, the Petrograd Soviet created an Executive Committee headed by N.S. Chkeidze, a Menshevik, to make its most important decisions.

2.5.2 *Policies*

In response to an unsuccessful request to the Provisional Government to absolve soldiers from potentially treasonous actions during the March Revolution, the Petrograd Soviet issued Order No. I (March 14) that granted them amnesty and stated that officers were to be elected by their units. It later issued Order No. II for units throughout the country. These decrees, hesitatingly approved later by the Provisional Government, caused a significant collapse of discipline in the armed forces.

2.6   LENIN RETURNS TO RUSSIA

Vladimir Ilyich Ulyanov (Lenin) (1870 – 1924) became involved in revolutionary activity after the execution of his brother for an assassination plot against Alexander III. A committed Marxist, he split with the Menshevik wing of the Russian Social Democratic Party and formed his "Bolshevik" (majority) faction in 1903. Lenin felt the party should be led by a committed elite. He spent much of the period between 1905 and 1917 in exile, and was surprised by the February Revolution. However, with the aid of the Germans, he and some followers were placed in a sealed train and transported from Switzerland via Stockholm to Russia.

2.6.1 *The April Theses*

On April 16, Lenin arrived at Petrograd's Finland Station and went into hiding. The next day, he proposed his April Theses to the city's Bolshevik leaders, who rejected them.

Lenin felt that the Bolsheviks should oppose the Provisional Government and support the theme "All Power to the Soviets." The Soviets, he concluded, should control the government while the war should become a revolution against capitalism, with all soldiers on both sides joining the struggle. In addition, the country's land, factories, and banks should be nationalized, and the Bolshevik Party should begin to call itself the Communist Party.

2.7   THE FIRST COALITION

Paul Miliukov's decision on May 1 to insure the Allies that his country would not sign a separate agreement with Germany and continue to fight until a "decisive victory" was won, caused public demonstrations that forced his resignation and the Lvov government to disavow his note. Since the Soviet now permitted its members to join the Provisional Government, a new one, known as the First Coalition, was formed under Prince Lvov that included nine non-socialists and six socialist representatives. Some of its more prominent members were: Alexander Kerensky, who now became Minister of War and the Navy; Victor Chernov, a leading Socialist Revolutionary, now Minister of Agriculture; M. I. Tereshchenko, previously Finance Minister, as Foreign Minister; and H. Tsereteli, the Menshevik leader and head of the Petrograd Soviet, as Minister of Posts and Telegraph. In many instances, the Coalition's new socialist members felt more loyal to the Petrograd Soviet than to the government itself.

2.8   THE JULY CRISES

Because of Allied pressure, the Provisional Government decided to mount an offensive on the Eastern Front to counter French military failures and mutinies on the Western Front.

2.8.1 *The July Offensive*

Kerensky, determined to revive the Russian army, toured the front to rally his forces, and created special "shock" battalions to lead them into battle. On July 1, Russian forces attacked the Austrians in the Lvov area of Galicia and initially scored some successes, though within 12 days the Russian advance was halted, and a week later, Austro-German troops began to push the Russians back. Their retreat turned into a panic and desertions became rampant. The Provisional Government restored the death penalty on July 25 to stop this rupture in discipline, though it did little to stop the army's collapse.

2.8.2 *The Second Coalition*

In the midst of the July Offensive, the First Coalition collapsed. On July 16, four Kadet members resigned because of the Coalition's decision to grant the Ukraine quasi-federal status, while several days later, Prince Lvov stepped down as Prime Minister over the land question and efforts to strengthen Soviet influence in the Cabinet. Alexander Kerensky became Prime Minister, and twice made cabinet changes between July 25 and August 6. On August 22, he announced that elections for the Constituent Assembly would be on November 25, and that it would open on December 11.

2.8.3 *The July Days*

Prompted by the failures of the July offensive and the resignation of Kadet ministers from the Cabinet, military units and workers mounted a spontaneous protest against the Provisional Government on July 16. After hesitating, the Bolsheviks agreed to lead the demonstrations, which saw over 500,000 march on the Tauride Palace, demanding that the Petrograd Soviet seize power. The Soviet leaders refused, and on July 18 troops loyal to the Provisional Government put the demonstrations down.

Afterwards, the government claimed that Bolshevik leaders were German agents, and tried to arrest them. Many top Bolsheviks, criticized for their failure to seize power and branded as spies, went underground or fled abroad.

2.9 THE SECOND COALITION AND THE KORNILOV AFFAIR

In an effort to rebuild support for his government, Kerensky decided to call a meeting of delegates representing numerous organizations from throughout the country in late August. The rifts that developed there led to the Kornilov Crisis several weeks later.

2.9.1 *The Moscow State Conference (August 26 – 28)*

In an effort to find an alternative base of support for the Petrograd Soviet before elections to the Constituent Assembly, Kerensky convened the Moscow State Conference on August 26.

Over 2,000 delegates, representing the Duma, the military, the Soviets, the professions and other groups, met in Moscow. The Bolsheviks opposed the meeting and responded with a general strike.

The conference accentuated the growing difference between Kerensky and the conservatives, who looked to the government's Commander-in-Chief, General Lavr Kornilov, as a leader. Kornilov represented elements who decried the collapse of military discipline and left the Moscow Conference convinced that Kerensky did not have the ability to restore order and stability to the nation and the military.

2.9.2 The Kornilov Affair

The mutual suspicion between Kerensky and Kornilov resulted in a series of indirect, unofficial negotiations between the two that ended in Kornilov's dismissal on September 9. Kornilov responded by ordering his Cossack and "Savage" divisions to march to Petrograd to stop a Bolshevik *coup*. The Petrograd Soviet rallied to save the revolution, and freed the Bolsheviks from prison to help with defense preparations. Kornilov's *coup* collapsed, and he surrendered on September 14. Kerensky now became Supreme Commander-in-Chief.

2.9.3 The Third Coalition

On September 14, Kerensky restructured his government as a temporary Directory of Five, and declared Russia a Republic. Thirteen days later, he convened a large gathering of 1,200 representatives from throughout the country to rebuild his power base. From it emerged a Third Coalition government on October 8, that consisted of Socialist Revolutionaries, Mensheviks, Kadets, and ministers without ties to any faction. The conference also decided to establish a Council of the Russian Republic or preparliament with 555 delegates that would open on October 20. The Bolsheviks and other leftists opposed these efforts, which weakened Kerensky's efforts.

2.10 THE BOLSHEVIK OCTOBER REVOLUTION

The Kornilov affair and Kerensky's failure to rebuild support for the Provisional Government convinced the Bolshevik's two leaders, Lenin and Leon Trotsky, that now was the time for them to attempt to seize power.

2.10.1 *Lenin's Decision to Seize Power*

After learning that the II All-Russian Congress of Soviets of Workers and Soldiers Deputies would open on November 7, Lenin began to think of a simultaneous seizure of power, since he was convinced that while the Bolsheviks could dominate that II Soviet Congress, they would not be able to do the same with the Constituent Assembly that was to open later. On October 23 – 24, he returned from Finland to meet with the Party's Central Committee to plan the *coup*. Though he met with strong resistance, the Committee agreed to create a Political Bureau (Politburo) to oversee the revolution.

2.10.2 *Trotsky and the Military Revolutionary Committee*

Leon Trotsky, head of the Petrograd Soviet and its Military Revolutionary Committee, convinced troops in Petrograd to support Bolshevik moves. While Trotsky gained control of important strategic points around the city, Kerensky, well-informed of Lenin's plans, finally decided on November 6 to move against the plotters.

2.10.3 *The Coup of November 6 – 7*

In response, Lenin and Trotsky ordered their supporters to seize the city's transportation and communication centers. The Winter Palace was captured later that evening, along with most of Kerensky's government.

2.10.4 *The II Congress of Soviets*

The II Congress opened at 11 p.m. on November 7, with Lev Kamenev, a member of Lenin's Politburo, as its head. Over half (390) of the 650 delegates were Bolshevik supporters, and its newly selected 22 member Presidium had 14 Bolsheviks on it. Soon after the II Congress opened, many of the moderate socialists walked out in opposition to Lenin's *coup*, leaving the Bolsheviks and the Left Socialist Revolutionaries in control of the gathering. Lenin now used the rump Congress as the vehicle to announce his regime.

At the Congress, it was announced that the government's new Cabinet, officially called the Council of People's Commissars (Sovnarkom), and responsible to a Central Executive Committee, would include Lenin as Chairman or head of government, Trotsky as Foreign Commissar, and Josef Stalin as Commissar of Nationalities. The Central Executive Committee of 101 (later 110) delegates would be the government's temporary legislature. The II Congress also issued two decrees on peace and land. The first called for immediate peace without any consideration of indemnities or annexations, while the second adopted the Socialist Revolutionary land program that abolished private ownership of land and decreed that a peasant could only have as much land as he could farm. Village councils would oversee distribution.

2.11   THE CONSTITUENT ASSEMBLY

The Constituent Assembly, long promised by the Provisional Government as the country's first legally elected legislature, presented serious problems for Lenin, since he knew the Bolsheviks could not win a majority of seats in it. Regardless, Lenin allowed elections for it to be held on November 25 under universal suffrage. Over 41,000,000 Russians voted. The SR's got 58% of the vote, the Bolsheviks 25%, the Kadets and other parties, 17%. The Assembly was to open on January 18, 1918, though for the next seven weeks, the Bolsheviks did everything possible to discredit the election results. When it convened on January 18 in the Tauride Palace, the building was surrounded by Red Guards and others. The Assembly voted down Bolshevik proposals and elected Victor Chernov, a Socialist Revolutionary, as president. The Bolsheviks walked out. After it adopted laws on land and peace, and declared the country a democratic federal republic, it was adjourned until the next day. When the delegates later returned to the Tauride Palace, they found it surrounded by troops, who announced that the Constituent Assembly was dissolved.

CHAPTER 3

WORLD WAR I: THE FINAL PHASE, 1917 – 1918

3.1 THE WESTERN FRONT, 1917

In early 1917, the new French commander, General Robert Nivelle, altered the earlier policy of attrition against the Germans, and began to plan distracting Somme attacks with a major assault against the Germans at Champagne. These plans caused friction with Field Marshal Douglas Haig, who had a different strategy and resented serving under Nivelle.

3.1.1 *The French Offensive*

The Champagne offensive began near Reims on April 16. By May 9, it failed at the second Battle of the Aisne. As a result, a series of mutinies broke out in the French army (May 3 – 20) that forced the replacement of Nivelle for Marshal Henri Petain, who restored order.

3.1.2   The British Offensive

To shore up the failing French battle effort, General Haig began a series of attacks in Flanders on June 7 that resulted in the capture of Messines Ridge the following day. Against French wishes, Haig began a new series of unsuccessful assaults (Third Battle of Ypres from July 31 to November 4) that were designed to capture the Flemish port cities of Ostend and Zeebrugge and ultimately failed. He did succeed in capturing the Passchendaele Ridge and seriously damaged the strength of the German 4th Army, though his own troops suffered heavy loses.

3.1.3   The Italian Front and the Battle of Caporetto

In response to increased Italian attacks against Austro-Hungary in the Isonzo area in August and September 1917, the German High Command decided to strengthen Central Power resistance with troops from the Eastern Front to defeat the Italians. Consequently, on October 24, a Central Power campaign began at Caporetto, which resulted in an Italian retreat through November 12 and the capture of 250,000 Italians. The loss convinced the Allies of the need to form a Supreme War Council at Versailles to enhance Allied cooperation.

3.1.4   The Tank Battle of Cambrai

From November 20 to December 3, the largest tank battle of the war took place at Cambrai involving 400 British tanks. After breaking through the German Hindenburg Line, a German counter offensive on November 30 pushed the British back.

3.2 THE MIDDLE AND NEAR EAST, 1917

3.2.1 *Mesopotamia*

The British revived their Mesopotamian campaign in 1917 and retook Al Kut on February 23. They captured Baghdad on March 11.

3.2.2 *Palestine*

British forces in Palestine unsuccessfully attacked Gaza on March 26 – 27, and reassaulted it with the same consequences on April 17 – 19. In the third offensive against Gaza from October 31 to November 7, Turkish forces retreated, which opened the way for a British attack on Jerusalem. While Col. T.E. Lawrence worked to stir Arab passions against the Turks, General Sir Edmund Allenby took Jerusalem on December 9 – 11.

3.3 THE U.S. ENTERS THE WAR

3.3.1 *American Neutrality*

Woodrow Wilson, the American President, issued a declaration of neutrality four days after war broke out in 1914, and offered to work to settle differences between both sides.

3.3.2 *The U.S. and Freedom of the Seas*

As the war expanded into the Atlantic, Allied efforts to stifle Central Power trade and the German use of the submarine created problems for the United States. In October 1914, President Wilson asked both sides to abide by the *Declaration of London* (1909) which laid out rules of actions and rights for neutrals and belligerents in war. Germany and its allies agreed to accept its terms because of their inferior naval strength, while the Allied powers refused.

3.3.3   Germany and Submarine Warfare

Throughout the latter part of 1915 and 1916, the U.S. was able to restrict most German submarine activity in the Atlantic because Berlin wanted to avoid any crisis that might bring America into the war. However, the failure of peace initiatives at the end of that year convinced German leaders, who felt their submarine fleet was now capable of a successful full blockade of England, to reinstitute unlimited submarine warfare in the Atlantic on January 31, 1917. Though they knew this policy would probably bring the U.S. into the war, they felt they could defeat Great Britain well before the U.S. could significantly alter its course.

3.3.4   *The Zimmerman Telegram*

On March 2, British intelligence published the Zimmerman Telegram, a note from the German Foreign Minister to his ambassador in Mexico that ordered him to seek an alliance with that country that would allow Mexico to seize the American Southwest if the U.S. entered the war. The message, which was revealed several days after a number of Americans died on the *Laconia* from a U-boat attack, helped – along with the creation of a democratic Provisional Government in Russia – convince the President and American public opinion that it was now time to enter the war, which the United States did on April 6, 1917.

3.4   RUSSIA LEAVES THE WAR

One of the cornerstones of Bolshevik propaganda throughout 1917 was a promise to end the war after they had seized power. Once in control, Soviet authorities issued a decree that called for immediate peace "with no indemnities or annexations" at the II Congress of Soviets on November 8, 1917.

3.4.1 *The Armistice at Brest-Litovsk*

As order among Russian units along the Eastern Front collapsed, the Soviet government began to explore cease fire talks with the Central Powers. Leon Trotsky, the Commissar of Foreign Affairs, offered general negotiations to all sides, and signed an initial armistice as a prelude to peace discussions with Germany at Brest-Litovsk on December 5, 1917.

3.4.2 *Trotsky and Initial Peace Negotiations with Germany*

Trotsky, who replaced Adolf Joffe as principal delegate soon after talks began, felt he could utter a few revolutionary phrases and close up shop. He was shocked by German demands for Poland, Lithuania and Kurland when negotiations opened on December 22, 1917, which prompted him to return to Moscow for consultations with the Bolshevik leadership.

3.4.3 *Soviet Differences Over Peace Terms*

Three different perspectives emerged over the German peace terms among the Soviet leadership:

1) One group, led by Nikokai Bukharin, wanted the conflict to continue as a revolutionary war designed to spread Bolshevism;

2) Lenin, however, felt the country needed peace for his government to survive. Western revolution would take place later;

3) Trotsky wanted a policy of no war and no peace.

At a Bolshevik meeting on January 21, 1918, the Soviet leadership barely selected Bukharin's proposal, while the Central Committee overrode this decision on January 24 in favor of Trotsky's proposal.

3.4.4 *Negotiations Resume at Brest-Litovsk*

Trotsky returned to the peace talks and tried to stall them with his no war, no peace theme. He left Brest-Litovsk on February 10, and eight days later, the Germans responded with broad attacks all across the Eastern Front that met with little Soviet opposition.

3.4.5 *The Soviet Response and the Treaty of Brest-Litovsk*

On the day the German offensive began, Lenin barely convinced Party leaders to accept Germany's earlier offer. Berlin responded with harsher ones, which the Soviets grudgingly accepted, and were integrated into the Treaty of Brest-Litovsk of March 3, 1918. According to its terms, in return for peace, Soviet Russia lost its Baltic provinces, the Ukraine, Finland, Byelorussia, and part of Transcaucasia. The area lost totalled 1,300,000 square miles and included 62 million people.

3.5 THE ALLIED BREAKTHROUGH

By the end of 1917, the Allied war effort seemed in disarray. The French and Italian governments had changed hands in an effort to revive war spirits, while an Anglo-French force arrived to stop the Central advance after Caporetto. To strengthen Allied resolves, the United States declared war on Austro-Hungary on December 6, 1917, while the Allies developed new mining policies to handicap German U-boat movements.

3.5.1 *The American Presence: Naval and Economic Support*

The United States, which had originally hoped that it could simply supply the Allies with naval and economic support, made their naval presence known immediately and helped Great Britain mount an extremely effective blockade of Germany and, through a convoy system, strengthened the shipment of goods across the Atlantic.

Despite the difficulties of building a military system from scratch, the United States was slowly able to transform its peacetime army of 219,665 men and officers into a force of 2 million. An initial token group, the American Expeditionary Force under General John J. Pershing, arrived in France on June 25, 1917, while by the end of April 1918, 300,000 Americans a month were placed as complete divisions alongside British and French units.

3.5.2 *The German Offensive of 1918*

Emboldened by their victory over Russia, the German High Command decided to launch an all-out offensive against the Allies in France to win the war.

The German Plan. Strengthened by forces from the Russian front, Erich Ludendorff, the Germans' principal war planner, intended to drive his divisions, which outnumbered the Allies 69 to 33, between the British and the French, and push the former to the Channel.

The German Attacks. Beginning on March 21, 1918, Ludendorff mounted four major attacks on the Allied forces in ʾnce: Somme (March 21 – April 4), Lys (April 9 – 29), (May 27 – June 6), and Champagne-Marne (July 15 – ʾ success of the assaults so concerned the Allies that they appointed the French Chief of Staff, Ferdinand Foch, Generalissimo of Allied Forces on April 14. In the third attack on Aisne, the Germans came within 37 miles of Paris. However, the increasing appearance of fresh, though untried American forces, combined with irreplaceable German manpower losses, began to turn the war against the Germans. Four days after the decisive German crossing of the Marne, Foch counterattacked and began to plan for an offensive against the Germans.

3.5.3   *The Allied Offensive of 1918*

Western Front. Stirred by the successes on the Marne, the Allies began their offensive against the Germans at Amiens on August 8, 1918. Ludendorff, who called this Germany's "dark day," soon began to think of ways to end the fighting. By September 3, the Germans retreated to the Hindenburg Line. On September 26, Foch began his final offensive, and took the Hindenburg Line the following day. Two days later, Ludendorff advised his government to seek a peace settlement. Over the next month, the French took St. Quetin (October 1), while the British occupied Cambrai, Le Cateau, and Ostend.

Macedonia. On September 14, Allied forces attacked in the Salonika area and forced Bulgaria to sue for peace on September 29.

Palestine. On September 19, General Allenby began an attack on Turkish forces at Megiddo and quickly defeated them. In a rapid collapse of Turkish resistance, the British took Damascus, Aleppo, and finally forced Turkey from the war at the end of October.

Italy. On October 24, the Italians began an assault against Austria-Hungary at Vitto Veneto and forced Vienna to sign armistice terms on November 3.

3.6   THE ARMISTICE WITH GERMANY

Several days after Ludendorff advised his government to seek peace, Prince Max of Baden assumed the German Chancellorship. On October 4, he asked President Wilson for an armistice, based on the American President's "Fourteen Points" of January 8, 1918. The Allies hesitatingly agreed to support the President's terms, with qualifications, which were given to the Germans on November 5. On November 11 at 11:00 a.m., the war ended on the Western Front.

3.7   THE COLLAPSE OF THE GERMAN MONARCHY AND THE CREATION OF THE GERMAN REPUBLIC

The dramatic collapse of German military fortunes had seriously undercut the credibility of the Kaiser, Wilhelm II, and strengthened the hand of the country's politicians. Stimulated by the growing threat of revolution after the German naval rebellion in Kiel on October 28, that had spread to the army, efforts were made to try to get the Kaiser to abdicate in hopes that this would enable Germany to receive better terms from the Allies. The Kaiser fled to army headquarters in Belgium, while on November 9 the Chancellorship was transferred to Friederich Ebert after his fellow socialist leader, Phillip Scheidemann, announced the creation of a German Republic on the same day.

CHAPTER 4

THE PARIS PEACE
CONFERENCE OF 1919 – 1920

4.1   WAR LOSSES AND THEIR IMPACT
ON THE PEACE CONFERENCE

To a very great extent, the direction and thrust of the discussions at the Paris Peace Conference were determined by the destructive nature of the war itself and the political responsibilities, ideals, and personalities of the principle architects of the settlements at Paris: President Woodrow Wilson of the United States, Prime Minister Lloyd George of Great Britain, Prime Minister/Minister of War Georges Clemenceau of France, and Prime Minister Vittorio Orlando of Italy.

As politicians, they reflected the general mood of victorious Europe's population, who wanted the principal Central Powers, Germany and Austria-Hungary, punished severely for this inhuman calamity. Total losses are not accurately known. Consequently, high and low estimates are given in some categories:

1) France: 1,500,000/1,363,000 dead and
4,797,800/4,660,800 wounded.

2) British Empire: 1,000,000/908,000 dead and
2,282,235/2,190,235 wounded.

3) Italy: 500,000/460,000 dead and
1,737,000/1,697,000 wounded.

4) United States: 116,708/100,000 dead and
104,000/87,292 wounded.

5) Russia: 1,700,000 dead and
7,450,000 wounded.

6) Germany: 2,000,000/1,774,000 dead and
5,368,558/5,142,588 wounded.

7) Austria-Hungary: 1,250,000/1,200,000 dead and
5,820,000/5,770,000 wounded.

4.2 WOODROW WILSON AND THE FOURTEEN POINTS

Not handicapped by significant financial or territorial concerns, Wilson idealistically promoted his Fourteen Points that he issued on January 8, 1918 – particularly the last, which dealt with a League of Nations – as the basis of the armistice and the peace settlement:

1) Open Covenants of Peace.

2) Freedom of the Seas.

3) Removal of Trade Barriers.

4) Arms Reduction.

5) Settlement of Colonial Claims.

6) Evacuation of Russia.

7) Restoration of Belgium.

8) Return of Alsace-Lorraine to France.

9) Adjustment of Italy's Borders along Ethnic Lines.

10) Autonomy for the Peoples of Austria-Hungary.

11) Evacuation and Restoration of the Balkans.

12) Autonomy for the Non-Turkish Parts of the Turkish Empire.

13) Independent Poland with an Outlet to the Sea.

14) League of Nations.

4.3 SECRET ALLIED AGREEMENTS CONCLUDED DURING WORLD WAR I

Throughout the war, the Allied powers had concluded a number of secret agreements designed to encourage countries to join their side or as compensation for war efforts. In March 1915, England and France had promised Russia Constantinople, the Straits, and the bordering areas as long as they were openly accessible. In April of the following year, England and France had promised one another, respectively, spheres in

Mesopotamia and Palestine, as well as Syria, Adana, Cilia, and southern Kurdistan. The Sykes-Picot Treaty in May 1916 better defined both countries' Arabian spheres. Russia was to have similar rights in Armenia, portions of Kurdistan, and northeastern Anatolia. The Allies gave Italy and Rumania significant territories to encourage them in their war effort in April 1915 and August 1916, while the English promised to support Japan's desire for Germany's Asian possessions. France and Russia agreed to promote one another's claims at a future peace conference, while Arab independence and creation of a Jewish homeland were also promised to others.

4.4 PRELIMINARY DISCUSSIONS

The sudden, unexpected end of the war, combined with the growing threat of communist revolution throughout Europe created an unsettling atmosphere at the conference. As a result of the Bolshevik victory in Russia, delegates from the United States, England, France, Italy, and later Japan, hurriedly began informal peace discussions on January 12, 1919. In time, this group was transformed into a Council of Ten, consisting of two representatives from each of these countries. This body conducted most of the significant talks in Paris until March 24, 1919, when the "Big Four" of Wilson (U.S.), Clemenceau (France), Lloyd-George (England), and Orlando (Italy) took over the discussions. Initially, the Allied Powers had hoped for a negotiated settlement with the defeated powers, which necessitated hard terms that would be negotiated down. However, the delays caused by uncertainty over direction at the beginning of the conference, Wilson's insistence that the League of Nations be included in the settlement, and fear of European-wide revolution resulted in a hastily prepared, dictated peace settlement.

4.4.1 *France and the Rhineland Conflict*

Once talks began among the Big Four, France insisted on the return of Alsace-Lorraine from Germany and the creation of an independent buffer state along the Rhine to protect it from Germany. The United States and Great Britain opposed these claims because they felt it could lead to future Franco-German friction. In return for an Allied guarantee of France's security against Germany, France got the Saar coal mines, and the demilitarization of the Rhine, with portions occupied by the Allies for fifteen years.

4.4.2 *German Disarmament*

Lloyd-George and Wilson saw German arms reductions as a prelude to a European-wide plan after the conference. They also opposed the draft, though agreed with the French about the need for a small German army.

4.4.3 *Reparations*

Each of the major powers had differing views on how much compensation Germany should pay for war indebtedness. At British insistence, civilian losses were added to the normal military ones. The "War Guilt" clause, Article 231, was included to justify heavy reparations, while the actual determination of the amount was left to a Reparations Commission.

4.5 THE TREATY OF VERSAILLES

The Treaty of Versailles, which was only between Germany and the Allied powers, had fifteen major sections, and almost 450 articles. Any country that ratified it, in turn accepted the League of Nations' Covenant in the first article:

1) Covenant of the League of Nations.

2) Boundaries of Germany.

3) Other Territories of Germany.

4) Germany's Overseas Boundaries and Rights.

5) Germany's Military and Naval Restrictions.

6) Prisoners of War.

7) War Guilt.

8) Reparations.

9) Costs of the War.

10) Customs Agreement and Other Covenants.

11) Aerial Navigation.

12) Freedom of Movement on Europe's Waterways.

13) Labor Organizations.

14) Guarantees.

15) Mandates for German Colonies and Other General Provisions.

4.5.1 *Most Significant Clauses*

War Guilt. The treaty's war guilt statements were the justification for its harsh penalties. The former German king, Wilhelm II, was accused of crimes against "international morality and the sanctity of treaties," while Germany took responsibility for itself and for its allies for all losses suffered by the Allied Powers and their supporters as a result of German and Central Power aggression.

Territorial Losses for Germany. Germany had to return Alsace and Lorraine to France and Eupen-Malmedy to Belgium. France got Germany's Saar coal mines as reparations, while the Saar Basin was to be occupied by the major powers for 15 years, after which a plebiscite would decide its ultimate fate. Poland got a number of German provinces and Danzig, now a free city, as its outlet to the sea.

Foreign Losses. Germany lost all of its colonies in Asia and Africa.

Military Reduction Classes. The German Army was limited to 100,000 men and officers with 12 year enlistments for the former and 25 for the latter. The General Staff was also abolished. The Navy lost its submarines and most offensive naval forces, and was limited to 15,000 men and officers with the same enlistment periods as the army. Aircraft and blimps were outlawed. A Reparations Commission was created to determine Germany's war debt to the Allies, which it figured in 1921 to be $31.4 billion, to be paid over an extended period of time. In the meantime, Germany was to begin immediate payments in goods and raw materials.

132 billion gold marks

4.5.2 German Hesitance to Sign the Treaty

The Allies presented the treaty to the Germans on May 7, 1919, but Foreign Minister Count Brockdorff-Rantzau refused to sign it, precipitating a crisis on both sides. The Germans were given a chance to reply to the voluminous document, which they did in-depth, constantly stating that its terms were too much for the German people, and that it violated the spirit of Wilson's Fourteen Points. After some minor changes were made, the Germans were told to sign the document or face an Allied advance into Germany. The treaty was signed on June 28, 1919, at Versailles.

4.6 TREATIES WITH GERMANY'S ALLIES

After the conclusion of the Treaty of Versailles, responsibility for concluding treaties with the other Central Powers fell on the shoulders of the Council of Foreign Ministers and later, the Conference of Ambassadors.

4.6.1 *The Treaty of St. Germain* (September 10, 1919)

The Allied treaty with Austria legitimized the breakup of the Austrian Empire in the latter days of the war and saw Austrian territory ceded to Italy and the new states of Czechoslovakia, Poland, and Yugoslavia. The agreement included military restrictions and debt payments.

4.6.2 *Treaty of Neuilly* (November 27, 1919)

Bulgaria lost territory to Yugoslavia and Greece and also had clauses on military limitations and reparations.

4.6.3 *Treaty of Trianon* (June 4, 1920)

The agreement with Hungary was delayed because of the communist revolution there in 1919 and Rumania's brief occupation of Budapest. Hungary lost two-thirds of its prewar territory in the agreement to Rumania, Yugoslavia, and Czechoslovakia, and became an almost purely Magyar nation. Reparations and military reduction terms were also in the accord.

4.6.4 *Treaty of Sevres* (August 10, 1920)

Turkey lost most of its non-Turkish territory, principally in the Middle and Near East, and saw the Straits and the surrounding area internationalized and demilitarized. The Turkish revolution of Mustafa Kemal Pasha ultimately saw its terms neutralized, and renegotiated, as the Treaty of Lausanne (July

24, 1923) with Turkey gaining territory in Anatolia, Smyrna, and Thrace.

4.7 PROBLEMS OF ALLIED UNITY: JAPAN, ITALY, AND THE U.S.

During and after the meetings in Paris that resulted in the Treaty of Versailles, disputes arose among the Allies that caused friction among them later.

4.7.1 *Japan*

During the treaty talks, Japan asked for Germany's Shantung Province in China, its Pacific colonies, and a statement on racial equality in the League Covenant. Japan got what it essentially wanted on the first two requests, despite protests from China on Shantung. However, Japan's request for a racial equality clause met strong opposition from the United States and some members of the British Commonwealth, who feared the impact of the statement on immigration. The proposal was denied, principally at the instigation of President Wilson.

4.7.2 *Italy*

The Italians came to Paris expecting full realization of the secret Treaty of London (1915), plus more. When Orlando proved stubborn on this matter, Wilson appealed directly to the Italian people on the issue on April 23, which prompted the Italian delegation temporarily to leave the conference. Italy got the Tyrol, as well as Istria and some Adriatic islands in the Treaty of Rapallo (December 12, 1920). Dalmatia, however, went to Yugoslavia, while Fiume was seized by the Italian patriot/poet Sabhiele D'Annunzio, on September 12, 1919. After a 14-month occupation he departed, leaving its destiny to Italy and Yugoslavia. The Treaty of Rome (January 27, 1924)

47

EUROPE AFTER WORLD WAR I

divided the city between the two, with Italy getting the lion's share of the area.

4.7.3   *The United States*

Although public and political sentiment was initially in favor of the treaty and its League provisions, Wilson's failure to include Senate representatives in the negotiating, and fear of Presidential usurpation of Congressional war powers helped create suspicions between Republicans and the President. This, and concern over the obligations of the United States in future European affairs, particularly those cited in Article X – which would, according to its opponents, give the United States no freedom of choice in deciding whether or not to intervene in world crises – prompted the Senate to reject it twice in 1919 and 1920, though by only seven votes on the latter occasion. The United States concluded a separate peace with Germany in 1921 and never joined the League, though it was active in some of its corollary organizations.

CHAPTER 5

POLITICAL DEVELOPMENTS IN POST-WAR EUROPE, 1918 – 1929

5.1 ENGLAND

Like most other European powers that emerged from the First World War, England had a set of problems unique to its status as a nation absolutely dependent on trade and commerce for its economic well-being.

5.1.1 *England, 1918 – 1922*

David Lloyd George and the Elections of 1918. With the war at an end, the Coalition government of David Lloyd George held the first parliamentary elections since 1910. Known as the "Coupon" or "Khaki" elections, the question of victory and the nature of the settlement with Germany and the Prime Minister himself were the election's burning issues. Before it took place, the Representation of the Peoples Act granted women over 30 the right to vote. Lloyd George and his

Conservative Coalition won a landslide victory (478 seats) while his opponents gained only 87.

The Economy. Afterwards, England enjoyed an economic boom fueled by government policies and economic production based on pre-war conditions. Unfortunately, government retrenchment, blended with tax increases and over production, resulted in a severe recession by the end of 1921. It began in 1920 with almost 700,000 unemployed by the end of that year and jumped to 2 million within months. Until the Depression, unemployment averaged 12% annually. This resulted in the passage of the Unemployment Insurance Acts (1920, 1922) for workers and the construction of 200,000 subsidized housing units.

The Irish Question. Triggered by the Easter Rebellion of 1916, the extremist Sinn Fein faction gained prominence in Ireland. In 1918, three quarters of its members elected to the British Parliament instead declared Irish independence in Dublin, which prompted a civil war between the Irish Republican Army and the Black and Tan, England's special occupation forces there. The Lloyd George government responded with a Home Rule division of Ireland with two legislatures, which only the northern six counties accepted. In October 1921, London created the Irish Free State, from which Ulster withdrew, as a part of the British Commonwealth.

5.1.2 *Politics, 1922 – 1924*

These problems caused the Conservatives to withdraw from Lloyd George's coalition. Andrew Bonar-Law replaced him as head of a new Conservative government, though ill health forced him to resign in 1923, followed briefly by Stanley Baldwin. Continued unemployment and labor problems, coupled with a decline to adopt more protectionistic trade policies resulted in a significant doctrine in support for the Conservatives in the elections of November 1923. Baldwin resigned, followed in office by Ramsey MacDonald, head of the Labour Party. His minority government only lasted nine months, and fell principally because of his efforts to establish formal ties with Russia.

5.1.3 *England and Stanley Baldwin, 1924 – 1929*

Baldwin entered his second Prime Ministership with a solid electoral victory (411 Seats) and strong Conservative Party backing. The year 1925 marked a turn in the economic crisis, with an increase in prices and wages. The country's return to the gold standard, which made the pound worth too much, affected British trade. In May 1926, a general strike in support of miners who feared a dramatic drop in their already low wages swept the country. Baldwin refused to concede to the miners' demands, broke the strike, and in 1927 sponsored the Trade Unions Act, which outlawed such labor action. On the other hand, the government passed a number of pieces of social legislation that further allowed support for housing construction and expanded pensions through its Widows', Orphans', and Old Age Pensions Act (1925). It also passed new legislation in 1928 that gave women the same voting privileges as men. In foreign affairs, Baldwin cancelled the 1924 commercial agreement with the Soviet Union, and, as a result of Soviet espionage activities, broke formal ties with the USSR in 1927.

5.2   FRANCE

The human losses in the war deeply affected France because of a population growth slowdown that had begun in the mid-19th century. Robbed of the flower of its youth, the Third Republic reflected in its political life and foreign policy a country ruled by an aging leadership that sought comfort in its rich past.

5.2.1 *The Bloc National, 1919 – 1924*

The election of November 1919 represented a momentary shift rightward with the moderate-conservatives winning almost two-thirds of the seats in the Chamber of Deputies. The new government, headed by Premier Alexandre Millerand, was a coalition known as the Bloc National. Aristide Briand replaced Millerand in January 1921, but was removed a year later because of lack of firmness on the German reparations question and was succeeded by Raymond Poincare.

Economic Policy. France had borrowed heavily during the war and spent great sums afterwards to rebuild its devastated economy. Unfortunately, it relied on German reparations to fund many of these costs. Problems with these repayments created a financial crisis that saw the French public debt increase accompanied by a steady decline in the value of the franc.

Germany and the Reparations Crisis. Growing Franco-German differences over Germany's willingness to meet its debt payments created friction between both countries and toppled the government of August Briand.

Occupation of the Ruhr. In December 1922, Poincare declared Germany in default on its reparations payments, and the following month, with Belgium, occupied the Ruhr. Efforts to obtain payments in kind via Franco-Belgium operation of the Ruhr's mines and factories failed because of a policy of passive resistance by German workers in the area. The Ruhr's occupiers gained little more financially in payments than they had through normal means, and found the cost of occupation expensive. Consequently, the French government had to raise taxes 20% to cover the cost of the occupation.

5.2.2 *The Cartel des Gauches, 1924 – 1926*

Poincare's Ruhr occupation policy had divided French voters, while tax increases helped defeat the Bloc National in the May 1924 elections, though it did gain 51% of the popular vote. A Radical/Socialist coalition, the Cartel des Gauches, had majority control of the Chamber. It selected Edouard Herriot, a Radical leader, as Premier, while Millerand continued as President, and Aristide Briand as Foreign Minister. Millerand's interference in policy questions forced his removal on June 10, 1924, with his successor, Gaston Doumergne serving as President until 1931.

The Economy. France's ailing economy was plagued by a declining franc and inflation. Herriot's efforts to raise direct taxes, force higher levies on the rich, and lower interest rates on government bonds met with radical opposition, which sought indirect tax increases and cuts in government expenditures. Herriot was removed from office on April 10, 1925, and replaced by Paul Painleve, who served for eight months.

Foreign Policy. Briand, who dominated French foreign affairs until 1932, pursued a policy of reconciliation with Germany and better relations with Europe's other pariah, the USSR. France granted diplomatic recognition to Soviet Russia in 1924, though relations quickly worsened because of the difficulty in getting the tsarist debt question resolved and the Soviets' use of their Paris embassy for espionage activities.

5.2.3 *The Union Nationale, 1926 – 1928*

The most crucial domestic problem faced by the Carte des Gauches was the declining franc, which by 1926 was only worth one-tenth of its prewar value. Its fall caused a political crisis so severe that the country had six cabinets over a nine month period. Consequently, on July 15, 1926, Briand resigned his premiership, succeeded by Poincare, who formed a Union National cabinet that had six former premiers in it. This coalition was backed by the Radicals as well as Conservatives and centrist parties in the legislature. To resolve the franc problem, the Chamber granted Poincare special authority. Over the next two years, he dramatically raised taxes and was able to get capital that had been taken out of the country reinvested in government bonds or other areas of the economy. By 1928, the franc had risen to 20% of its prewar value, and Poincare was considered a financial miracle worker. Unfortunately, the political and psychological scars left by the crisis would haunt France for two more decades.

5.3 WEIMAR GERMANY, 1918 – 1929

The dramatic collapse of the German war effort in the second half of 1918 ultimately created a political crisis that forced the abdication of the King and the creation of a German Republic on November 9.

5.3.1 *Provisional Government*

From the outset, the Provisional Government, formed of a coalition of Majority and Independent Socialists, was beset by divisions from within and threats of revolution throughout Germany. The first Chancellor was Friedrich Ebert, the Majority Socialist leader. On November 22, state leaders agreed to support a temporary government until elections could be held for a nationally elected legislature, which would draw up a constitution for the new republic.

Elections and Formation of the Weimar Republic. Elections for the new National Constituent Assembly, which was to be based on proportional representation, gave no party a clear majority. A coalition of the Majority Socialists, the Catholic Center Party, and the German Democratic Party

GERMANY AFTER WORLD WAR I

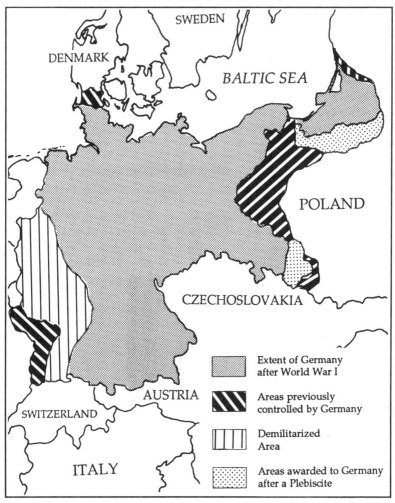

(DDP) dominated the new assembly. On February 11, 1919, the assembly met in the historic town of Weimar and selected Friedrich Ebert President of Germany. Two days later, Phillip Scheidermann formed the first Weimar Cabinet and became its first Chancellor.

The Weimar Constitution. On August 11, 1919, a new constitution was promulgated, which provided for a bicameral legislature. The upper chamber, the Reichsrat, represented the Federal states, while the lower house, the Reichstag, with 647 delegates elected by universal suffrage, supplied the country's Chancellor and Cabinet. A President was also to be elected separately for a 7-year term. As a result of Article 48 of the Constitution, he could rule through emergency decree, though the Reichstag could take this authority from him.

5.3.2   *Problems of the Weimar Republic, 1919 – 1920*

Domestic Problems. The new government faced a number of serious domestic problems that severely challenged or undercut its authority. Its forced acceptance of the hated *Friedensdiktat* ("the dictated peace") seriously undermined its prestige, while the unsuccessful, though violent Communist Spartikist Rebellion (January 5 – 11, 1919) in Berlin created a climate of instability. This was followed three months later by the brief communist takeover of Bavaria, and the rightist Kapp Putsch (March 13 – 17, 1920) in the capital the following year.

The Economic Crisis. The territorial, manpower, and economic losses suffered during and after the war, coupled with a $30.4 billion reparations debt, had a severe impact on the German economy and society, and severely handicapped the new government's efforts to establish a stable governing environment:

1) *The Inflation Crisis.* In an effort of good faith based on hopes of future reparation payment reductions, Germany borrowed heavily and made payments in kind to fulfill its early debt obligations. The result was a spiral of inflation later promoted by the Weimar government to underline Allied insensitivity to Germany's plight, that saw the mark go from 8.4 to the dollar in 1919 to

7,000 marks to the dollar by December 1922. After the Allied Reparations Commission declared Germany in default on its debt, the French and the Belgians occupied the Ruhr on January 11, 1923.

2) *The German Response to the Ruhr Occupation.* Chancellor Wilhelm Cuno encouraged the Ruhr's Germans passively to resist the occupation, and printed worthless marks which dropped from 40,000 to the dollar in January 1923 to 4.2 trillion to the dollar eleven months later. The occupation ended on September 26, and helped prompt stronger Allied sympathy to Germany's payment difficulties, though the inflationary spiral had severe economic, social, and political consequences.

5.3.3   *Weimar Politics, 1919 – 1923*

Germany's economic and social difficulties deeply affected its infant democracy. From February 1919 to August 1923, the country had six Chancellors.

Reichstag Elections of 1920. In the aftermath of the Kapp Putsch, conservative demands for new elections resulted in a June defeat for the ruling coalition that saw the Democrats (DDP) lose seats to the German National People's Party (DVP) headed by Gustav Stresemann, and the Majority Socialists lose seats to the more reactionary Independent socialists. Conservative Germans blamed the Weimar Coalition for the hated Versailles "Diktat" with its war guilt and reparations terms, while leftist voters felt the government had forgotten its social and revolutionary ideals.

Assassinations by the Right. Growing right-wing discontent with the Weimar Government resulted in the assassination of the gifted head of the Catholic Center Party, Matthias

Erzberger, on August 29, 1921, and the murder of Foreign Minister Walter Rathenau on June 24, 1922. These were two of the most serious of over 350 political murders in Germany since the end of the war.

5.3.4   *The Policies of Gustav Stresemann*

The dominant figure in German politics from 1923 to 1929 was Gustav Stresemann, the founder and leader of the DVP. Though he served as Chancellor from August 12 to November 23, 1923, his prominence derives from his role as Foreign Minister from November 1923 until his death on October 3, 1929. He received the Nobel Peace Prize for his diplomatic efforts in 1926.

Stresemann's Chancellorship. As Chancellor, he felt that the only road to recovery and treaty revision lay in adherence to the Versailles settlement and positive relations with France and its allies. Consequently, on September 26, he ended passive resistance in the Ruhr and began to search for a solution to Germany's reparations payment problem with France. To restore faith in the currency, the government introduced a new one, the *Rentenmark*, on November 20, 1923, that was equal to 1 billion old marks, and was backed by the mortgage value of Germany's farm and industrial land.

The Dawes Plan (April 9, 1924). In an effort to come up with a more reasonable debt payment plan for Germany, the Western Allies developed the Dawes Plan that accepted the need for Germany to pay its war debts and blended England's desire for balance with France's needs for repayment assurances. According to its terms, Germany was to begin small payments of a quarter of a billion dollars annually for four years, to be increased if its economy improved. In return, the Allies agreed to help revitalize Germany's ailing economy with a $200 million American loan and withdrawal from the Ruhr.

The Locarno Pact (December 1, 1925). The crowning achievement in Stresemann's efforts to restore Germany to normal status in the European community was the Locarno Pact of 1925.

5.3.5 *Weimar Politics, 1924 – 1928*

1924 Elections. Reichstag elections were held twice in 1924. The May 4 contest reflected a backlash against the country's economic difficulties, and saw the Communists win 3,700,000 votes and the Nazis almost 2 million, at the expense of the moderate parties. The December 7 elections were something of a vote on the Dawes Plan and economic revival, and saw the Nazis and the Communists lose almost a million votes apiece.

1925 Presidential Elections. Following the death of President Ebert on February 28, two ballots were held for a new President, since none of the candidates won a majority on the first vote. On the second ballot on April 26, the *Reichsblock*, a coalition of Conservative parties, was able to get its candidate, war hero Paul von Hindenburg, elected narrowly against a Centrist coalition and the communists, who had a much smaller showing. Hindenburg, who some conservatives hoped would turn the clock back, vowed to uphold Weimar's Constitution.

Reichstag Elections of 1928. The elections of May 20, 1928, saw the Social Democrats get almost one-third of the popular vote which, blended with other moderate groups, created a stable moderate majority in the Reichstag, which chose Hermann Muller as Chancellor. The Nazis, who held 14 Reichstag seats at the end of 1924, lost one, while Communist strength increased.

5.4 ITALY

Like other countries that had fought in the World War, Italy had suffered greatly and gained little. Its economy, very weak even before the war broke out, relied heavily upon small family agriculture which contributed 40% of the country's GNP in 1920. Consequently, many of the social, political, and economic problems that plagued the country after the war cannot be blamed solely on the conflict itself.

5.4.1 *Italian Politics, 1918 – 1919*

As a result of growing discontent over the country's troubled economy, the Italian public looked to the parties that offered the most reasonable solutions. Strengthened by universal suffrage, and new proportional representation in Parliament, the Socialists doubled the number of seats to 156 in the Chamber of Deputies in the elections of November 16, 1919, while the new Catholic People's Party gained 99 positions. The former party had little faith in the current state, and longed for its downfall, while the latter mixed conservative religious ideals with a desire for political moderation. Most important, no strong majority coalition emerged in this or the Parliament elected in May 1921 that was able to deal effectively with the country's numerous problems.

5.4.2 *Government of Giovanni Giolitti, 1920 – 1921*

From June 9, 1920 until June 26, 1921, Italy's Premier was Giovanni Giolitti, a gifted musician and pre-war figure who had dominated Italian politics between 1901 and 1914. His tactics, to resolve Italy's international conflicts and stay aloof of its domestic conflicts, exacerbated the country's problems. The Socialists took advantage of this atmosphere and promoted a series of strikes and other labor unrest in August and September 1920 that became violent and divided the country and the

Socialist movement. Giolitti let the strikes run their course, and worked successfully to lower the government's deficit by 50%.

5.4.3 *Benito Mussolini and Italian Fascism*

Mussolini's Background. Benito Mussolini, named by his Socialist blacksmith father after the Mexican revolutionary, Benito Juarez, was born in 1883. After a brief teaching stint, he went to Switzerland to avoid military service but returned and became active in Socialist politics. In 1912, he became editor of the Party's newspaper, *Avanti.* Several months after the outbreak of the World War, he broke with the party over involvement in the war, and began to espouse nationalistic ideas that became the nucleus of his fascist movement. He then opened his own newspaper, *Popolo d'Italia* (The People of Italy) to voice his ideas. Mussolini was drafted into military service in 1915, and badly wounded two years later. After recuperating, he returned to his newspaper, where he blended his feelings about socialism and nationalism with an instinct for violence.

Mussolini and Early Post-War Italy. Italy's post-war conflict with its allies at the Paris Peace conference over fulfillment of the terms of the 1915 Treaty of London and the additional request for Fiume played into Mussolini's hands. Mussolini supported the D'Annunzio coup there.

Formation of the Fascist Movement. Mussolini, capitalizing on the sympathy of unfulfilled war veterans, disaffected nationalists, and those fearful of communism, formed the *Fascio di combattimento* (Union of Combat) in Milan on March 23, 1919. Initially, Mussolini's movement had few followers, and it did badly in the November 1919 elections. However, Socialist strikes and unrest enabled him to convince Italians that he alone could bring stability and prosperity to their troubled country.

Growth of Fascist Power. Fascism's most significant growth came in the midst of the Socialist unrest in 1920. Strengthened by large contributions from wealthy industralists, Mussolini's black-suited *Squadristi* attacked Socialists, communists, and ultimately, the government itself. Mussolini's followers won 35 seats in the legislative elections in May 1921, which also toppled the Giolitti cabinet.

Formation of the Fascist Party. The center of Fascist strength was in the streets of northern Italy, which Mussolini's followers, through violence, came to control. Mussolini now transformed his movement into the Fascist Party, dropped his socialist views, and began to emphasize the predominance of Italian nationalism.

Mussolini Seizes Power. The resignation of the Bonomi Cabinet on February 9, 1922, underlined the government's inability to maintain stability. In the meantime, the Fascists seized control of Bologna in May and Milan in August. In response, Socialist leaders called for a nationwide strike on August 1, 1922, which Fascist street violence stopped in 24 hours. On October 24, 1922, Mussolini told followers that if he was not given power, he would "March on Rome." Three days later, Fascists began to seize control of other cities, while 26,000 began to move towards the capital. The government responded with a declaration of martial law, which the king, Victor Emmanuel III, refused to approve. On October 29, the king asked Mussolini to form a new government as Premier of Italy.

5.4.4 *Mussolini's Consolidation of Power*

Using tactics similar to those of D'Annunzio to seize Fiume earlier, Mussolini built a government made up of a number of sympathetic parties.

The Cabinet and Parliament. Mussolini formed a coalition cabinet that included all major parties except the Communists and the Socialists. After he assured the Chamber of Deputies that his government intended to respect personal liberties but with "dignity and firmness...," it approved his government in a 306 to 116 vote. Nine days later, the Chamber granted him quasi-dictatorial powers for a year.

Acerbo Election Law and Transformation of the Government. To enhance his political control of the government, one of Mussolini's assistants, Giacomo Acerbo, successfully introduced a bill to the Chamber on July 21, 1923 (later approved by the Senate) that stated that the party that got the largest number of votes in a national election with a minimum of 25% of the votes cast would control two-thirds of the seats in the Chamber. Mussolini also began to remove non-Fascists from his Cabinet, the Civil Service, and other organs of government. The king kept his throne though Mussolini now became Head of State.

Elections of 1924. In violence-marred elections on April 6, 1924, the Fascists gained 60% of the popular vote and two-thirds of the Chamber's seats. In response to Fascist campaign tactics, Giacomo Matteotti, a Socialist Chamber member, attacked the Fascists for their misdeeds on May 30. Several days later, Fascist supporters kidnapped and murdered him, provoking his supporters, unwisely, to walk out of the Chamber in protest. Momentarily, Italy was stunned, and Mussolini was vulnerable. The opposition asked the king to dismiss Mussolini, but he refused.

5.4.5 Consolidation of the Dictatorship

On January 3, 1925, Mussolini accepted responsibility for events of the past year, and warned that this instability, caused by his opponents, would be quickly resolved. What followed was a new reign of terror that arrested opponents, closed news-papers, and eliminated basic civil liberties for Italians. On December 24, 1925, the legislature's powers were greatly limited, while those of Mussolini were increased as the new Head of State. Throughout 1926, Mussolini intensified his control over the country with legislation that outlawed strikes and created the syndicalist corporate system. A failed assassination attempt prompted the "Law for the Defense of the State" of November 25, 1926, that created a Special Court to deal with political crimes and introduced the death penalty for threats against the king, his family or the Head of State.

5.4.6 *The Fascist Party*

In December 1922, Mussolini created a Grand Council of Fascism made up of the Party's principle leaders, with the Duce as its head. In 1928, the Grand Council became the most important organ of government in Italy. The structure of the Fascist Party did not reach final form until November 12, 1932. It was defined as a "civil militia" with the Duce (Mussolini) as its head. Its day-to-day affairs were run by the National Directorate headed by a Secretary, with two Vice Secretaries, an Administrative Secretary, and six other members. The Secretary of the National Directorate belonged to the Grand Council. The Party's Provincial Secretaries, appointed by Mussolini, oversaw local Party organizations, the *Fasci di Combattimento*. There were also separate Fascist youth organizations such as the *Piccole Italiane* (under 12) and the *Giovane Italiane* (over 12) for girls; the *Balilla* (8 – 14), the *Avanguardisti* (14 – 18), and the *Giovani Fascisti* (18 – 21) for boys. After 1927, only those who had been members of the *Balilla* and the *Avanguardisti* could be Party members.

5.4.7 *The Syndicalist-Corporate System*

In an effort to institutionalize his theories about relations between labor and management, Mussolini began to adopt some of the syndicalist theories of his followers. What emerged was a legal superstructure of labor-employer syndicates followed later by a series of government coordinated corporations to oversee the economy.

The Syndicates. On April 3, 1926, the Rocco Labor Law created syndicates or organizations for all workers and employers in Italy. It also outlawed strikes and walkouts. Later altered, it created nine syndicate corporations: four for workers and four for employers in each of the major segments of the economy and a ninth for professionals and artists.

Corporations. On July 1, 1926, Corporations were created to coordinate activities between the worker-employer syndicates, while later that year a Ministry of Corporations came into existence. On February 5, 1934, a Law on Corporations created 22 such bodies that oversaw every facet of the economy, coordinated management-labor relations, and economic production and shipment in every segment of the economy. Each Corporation was overseen by a Minister or other important government or Party official, who sat on the National Council of Corporations that was headed by Mussolini.

5.4.8 *Foreign Policy*

Some have called the first decade of Mussolini's reign the "time of good behavior." This was more because of his deep involvement in domestic affairs than his creative desire for foreign stability. This, plus the nation's wish for post-war peace and stability saw Italy participate in all of the international developments in the 1920's aimed at securing normalcy in relations with its neighbors.

Fiume. Because Italy did not receive its desired portions of Dalmatia at the Paris Peace Conference, Italian Nationalist

Gabriele D'Annunzio seized Fiume on the Adriatic in the fall of 1919. D'Annunzio's daring gesture as well as his deep sense of Italian national pride deeply affected Mussolini. However, in the atmosphere of detente prevalent in Europe at the time, he agreed to settle the dispute with Yugoslavia in a treaty on January 27, 1924, which ceded most of the port to Italy, and the surrounding area to Yugoslavia.

Corfu Incident. In the fall of 1923, Mussolini used the assassination of Italian officials working to resolve a Greek-Albanian border dispute to seize the island of Corfu, which he hoped to keep. Within a month, however, the British and the French convinced him to return the island for an indemnity.

5.5   SOVIET RUSSIA

Soon after the Bolshevik seizure of power, opposition forces began to gather throughout Russia that sought to challenge Soviet authority or use the occasion to breakup the Russian Empire.

5.5.1   *Origins of the Russian Civil War, 1918*

The Chelyabinsk Incident. After Brest-Litovsk, Lenin's government agreed to ship part of a large group of Czech POW's through Vladivostok to the Western Front. On May 14, 1918, a brawl took place between these units and Hungarian POW's at Chelyabinsk in the Urals that led to a Czech rebellion against Soviet authorities and the seizure of the Urals area and eastern Siberia by late summer.

The Allied Response and Intervention. In the spring of 1918, Russia's old war allies had begun to land forces in Russia at major shipping points such as Murmansk, Archangel, and Vladivostok to protect supplies they had sent the Provisional Government. The Czech rebellion stirred the Allied leaders meeting at Paris to upgrade their efforts in Russia to aid the Czechs and other Communist opponents in a limited, and hopefully, non-combative manner. They began to land limited military contingents at the above ports, at Baku and in Odessa to support a victor that would revive the Eastern Front, and to a lesser degree, counterbalance Lenin's threatening communist movement.

Formation of the "White" Resistance. Opposition to the Soviet takeover had begun immediately after Lenin's seizure of Petrograd. General M.V. Alexeev had formed a Volunteer Army, whose command was shared and later taken over by General Anton Denikin, who fled to the Don area in early 1918. Another center of White resistance was created first by Socialist Revolutionaries at Omsk, followed later by a government there under Admiral Alexander Kolchak, who was backed by Czech forces, and would declare himself Supreme Commander of White forces in the Civil War. In time, most of the major White Commanders would recognize Kolchak's authority. General Eugene Miller created a White opposition outpost at Archangel, and General Nicholas Yudenich another in Estonia.

The Soviet Buildup. To meet these threats, Lenin appointed Leon Trotsky as Commissar of War on March 13, 1918, with orders to build a Red Army. By the end of the year, using partial conscription, the new Soviet forces began to retake some of the areas earlier captured by the Whites.

5.5.2 *The Russian Civil War, 1919 – 1920*

Major Military Operations, 1919. The White forces, constantly weakened by lack of unified command and strategy, enjoyed their greatest successes in 1919, when Deniken, operating from the south, took Kharkov and later Odessa and Kiev. On the other hand, Yudenich was driven from Petrograd, while

Deniken lost Kharkov and Kiev. Kolchak had been defeated earlier, and Omsk was taken by November.

Major Military Operations, 1920. By early 1920, White fortunes had begun to collapse. On January 4, Kolchak abdicated in favor of Denikin, and was turned over by his Czech protectors to the Soviets, who executed him on February 7. In the meantime, Denikin's capital, Rostov, was taken by the Red Army and his command was taken over later by General Peter Wrangel, whose forces were beaten that fall. Both armies were evacuated from the Crimea.

The Polish-Soviet War, 1920. The new Polish state under Marshal Joszef Pilsudski sought to take advantage of the Civil War in Russia to retake territory lost to Russia during the Polish Partitions in the late 18th century. Polish forces invaded the Ukraine on April 25, and took Kiev two weeks later. A Soviet counteroffensive reached Warsaw by mid-August, but was stopped by the Poles. Both sides concluded an armistice on October 12 and signed the Treaty of Riga on March 12, 1921, that placed Poland's border east of the Curzon Line.

5.5.3 Domestic Policy and Upheaval, 1918 – 1921

War Communism. In order to provide more food to Russia's cities, the Soviet government implemented a "War Communism" program that centered around forced grain seizures and class war between "Kulaks" (ill-defined middle class peasants) and others. All major industry was also nationalized. These policies triggered rebellions against the seizures that saw the amount of land under cultivation and the total grain produced drop between 1918 – 1921.

Kronstadt Rebellion. The Civil War and War Communism had brought economic disaster and social upheaval throughout the country. On March 1, 1921, as the Soviet leadership met to decide on policies to guide the country in peace, a naval rebellion broke out at the Kronstadt naval base. The Soviet leadership sent Trotsky to put down the rebellion, which he did brutally by March 18.

5.5.4 *The New Economic Policy, 1921 – 1927*

The Kronstadt rebellion strengthened Lenin's resolve to initiate new policies approved at the X Party Congress that would end grain seizures and stimulate agricultural production. Termed the New Economic Policy (NEP), the government maintained control over the "Commanding Heights" of the economy (foreign trade, transportation, and heavy industry) while opening other sectors to limited capitalist development. It required the peasants to pay the government a fixed acreage tax, and allowed them to sell the surplus for profit. Once the government had resolved the inconsistencies in agricultural and industrial output and pricing, the NEP began to near 1913 production levels. The country remained dominated by small farms and peasant communes. Industrial production also improved, though it was handicapped by outdated technology and equipment which would hinder further output or expansion beyond 1913 levels.

5.5.5 *The Death of Lenin and the Rise of Josef Stalin*

Vladimir Ilyich Lenin, the founder of the Soviet State, suffered a serious stroke on May 26, 1922 and a second in December of that year. At this point, as he faced possible forced retirement or death, he composed a secret "testament" that surveyed the strengths and weaknesses of his possible successor, Stalin, who he feared would abuse power. Unfortunately, his third stroke prevented him from removing Stalin from his position as General Secretary. Lenin died on January 21, 1924.

Josef Stalin (1879 – 1953). Josef Visarionovich Dzugashvili was born in the Georgian village of Gori in 1879. He became involved in Lenin's Bolshevik movement in his 20's and became Lenin's expert on minorities. Intimidated by the Party's intellectuals, he took over numerous, and in some cases, seemingly unimportant Party organizations after the Revolution and transformed them into important bases of power. Among them were *Politburo* (Political Bureau), which ran the country; the *Orgburo* (Organizational Bureau), which Stalin headed, and which appointed people to positions in groups that implemented Politiburo decisions; the *Inspectorate* (Rabkrin, Commissariat of the Workers' and Peasants' Inspectorate), also under Stalin's control, which tried to eliminate Party corruption; and the *Secretariat*, which worked with all Party organs and set the Politburo's agenda. Stalin served as the Party's General Secretary after 1921.

Leon Trotsky (1879 – 1940). Lev Davidovich Bronstein (Trotsky) was a Jewish intellectual active in Menshevik revolutionary work, particularly in the 1905 Revolution. He joined Lenin's movement in 1917, and soon became his right-hand man. He was Chairman of the Petrograd Soviet, headed the early Brest-Litovsk negotiating team, served as Foreign Commissar, and was father of the Red Army. A brilliant organizer and theorist, Trotsky was also brusque and, some felt, overbearing.

5.5.6   *The Struggle for Power, 1924 – 1925*

The death of Lenin in 1924 intensified a struggle for control of the Party between Stalin and Trotsky and their respective supporters. Initially, the struggle, which began in 1923, appeared to be between Kamenev, head of the Moscow Soviet, and Zinoviev, Party chief in Petrograd and head of the Comintern, and Trotsky. The former two, allied with Stalin, presented a formidable opposition group to Trotsky.

Trotsky and "Permanent Revolution." Initially, the struggle centered around Trotsky's accusation that the trio was drifting away from Lenin's commitment to the revolution and "bureaucratizing" the Party. Trotsky believed in the theory of "permanent revolution" that blended an ongoing commitment to world revolution and building socialism with the development of a heavy industrial base in Russia.

Stalin and "Socialism in One Country." Stalin responded with the concept of "Socialism in One Country," that committed the country to building up its socialist base regardless of the status of world revolution.

Trotsky and "Lessons of October." In the fall of 1924, Trotsky attacked Zinoviev and Kamenev for the drift away from open discussion in the Party and for not supporting Lenin's initial scheme to seize power in November 1917. As a result, Trotsky was removed as Commissar of War on January 16, 1925, while two months later the Party accepted "Socialism in One Country" as its official governing doctrine.

5.5.7 *The Struggle for Power, 1925 – 1927*

Stalin and the Right. Zinoviev and Kamenev, who agreed with the principles of "Permanent Revolution," began to fear Stalin and soon found themselves allied against him and his new Rightist supporters, Nikolai Bukharin, Alexis Rykov, Chairman of the Council of People's Commisars (Cabinet), and Mikhail Tomsky, head of the trade unions.

The XIV Party Congress rebuffed Kamenev and Zinoviev, and accepted Bukharin's economic policies. It demoted Kamenev to candidate status on the Politburo, while adding a number of Stalin's supporters to that body as well as the Central Committee. Afterwards, Kamenev and Zinoviev joined Trotsky in their dispute with Stalin. As a result, Trotsky and Kamenev lost their seats on the Politburo, while Zinoviev was removed as head of the Comintern.

The Thermidorian Reaction. In early 1927, Trotsky and his followers accused Stalin and the Right of a "Thermidorian Reaction," Menshevism, and criticized recent foreign policy failures in England and China. Trotsky and Zinoviev lost their positions on the Central Committee, which prompted them to participate in anti-Rightist street demonstrations on November 7, 1927. Both were then thrown out of the Party, followed by their supporters. Trotsky was forced into external exile in Central Asia, while Zinoviev and Kamenev, humiliated and defeated, begged successfully to be allowed to return to the fold.

Stalin Defeats the Right. At the XV Party Congress, Stalin indicated that the Party would now begin gradually to collectivize the country's predominantly small-farm agricultural system. His shocked Rightist allies, now outnumbered by Stalinists on the Politburo, sought an uncomfortable alliance with the defeated Left. Over the next two years, the major old Rightist allies of Stalin, Bukharin, Rykov, and Tomsky, lost their Politburo seats and other Party positions, and ultimately, their Party membership. Brief exile followed in some cases.

5.5.8 *Soviet Constitutional Development*

Soviet Russia adopted two constitutions in 1918 and 1924. The first reflected the ideals of the state's founders and created the Russian Soviet Federative Socialist Republic (RSFSR) as the country's central administrative unit. An All-Russian Congress of Soviets was the government's legislative authority, while a large Central Executive Committee (CEC), aided by a cabinet or Council of People's Commissars (Sovnarkom) wielded executive power. The Communist Party was not mentioned in the 1918 constitution or in the 1924 constitution. The 1924 document was similar to the earlier one, but also reflected the changes brought about by the creation of the Union of Soviet Socialist Republics (USSR) two years earlier. The CEC was divided into a Council of the Union and a Council of Nationalities, while a new Supreme Court and Procurator was added to the governmental structure. A similar political division was duplicated on lower administrative levels throughout the country. The new constitution also created a Supreme Court and a Procurator responsible to the CEC.

5.5.9   Foreign Policy, 1918 – 1929

Soviet efforts after the October Revolution to openly foment revolution throughout Europe and Asia, its refusal to pay Tsarist debts, and international outrage over the murder of the royal family in 1919 isolated the country. However, adoption of the NEP required more integration with the outside world to rebuild the broken economy.

Relations with Germany. Russia and Germany, Europe's post-World War I pariahs, drew closer out of necessity. By the early 1920's, Russia was receiving German technological help in weapons development while the Soviets helped train German pilots and others illegally. On April 16, 1922, Soviet Russia and Germany agreed to cancel their respective war debts and to establish formal diplomatic relations.

Relations with Great Britain. By 1921, the British concluded a trade accord with the Soviet government and in 1924 extended formal diplomatic recognition to the USSR. Strong public reaction to this move, coupled with the publication of the "Zinoviev Letter" of unknown origin helped topple the pro-Soviet MacDonald government, because the letter encouraged subversion of the British government. Relations were formally severed in 1927 because of Communist support of a British coal mine strike, discovery of spies in a Soviet trade delegation, and Soviet claims that it hoped to use China as a means of hurting England.

Relations with Asia. The Soviets worked to consolidate their sphere-of-influence acquired earlier in Mongolia, and helped engineer the creation of an independent, though strongly pro-Soviet, People's Republic of Mongolia in 1924.

In China, in an effort to protect traditional Asian strategic interests and take advantage of the chaotic "war lord" atmosphere in China, the Soviets helped found a young Chinese Communist Party (CCP) in 1921. However, when it became apparent that Sun Yat-sen's revolutionary Kuomintang (KMT) was more mature than the infant CCP, the Soviets encouraged an alliance between its Party and this movement. Sun's successor, Chiang Kai-shek, was deeply suspicious of the Communists and made their destruction part of his effort militarily to unite China.

Comintern (Third International or Communist International). Founded in 1919, the Soviet-controlled Comintern sought to coordinate the revolutionary activities of communist parties abroad, though it often conflicted with Soviet diplomatic interests. It became an effectively organized body by 1924, and was completely Stalinized by 1928.

CHAPTER 6

EUROPE IN CRISIS: DEPRESSION AND DICTATORSHIP, 1929 – 1935

6.1 ENGLAND

6.1.1 *Ramsay MacDonald and the Depression, 1929 – 1931*

Required by law to hold elections in 1929, the May 30 contest saw the Conservatives drop to 260 seats, Labour rise to 287, and the Liberals 59. Ramsay MacDonald formed a minority Labour government that would last until 1931. The most serious problem facing the country was the Depression, which caused unemployment to reach 1,700,000 by 1930 and over 3 million, or 25% of the labor force, by 1932. To meet growing budget deficits caused by heavy subsidies to the unemployed, a special government commission recommended budget cuts and tax increases. Cabinet and labor union opposition helped reduce the total for the cuts (from 78 million to 22 million), but this could not help restore confidence in the government, which fell on August 24, 1931.

6.1.2 *The "National Government," 1931 – 1935*

The following day, King George VI helped convince MacDonald to return to office as head of a National Coalition cabinet made up of 4 Conservatives, 4 Laborites, and 2 Liberals. The Labour Party refused to recognize the new government and ejected MacDonald and Snowden from the Party. MacDonald's coalition swept the November 1931 general elections winning 554 of 615 seats.

Economic Policies. The British government abandoned the gold standard on September 21, 1931, and adopted a series of high tariffs on imports. Unemployment peaked at 3 million in 1932 and dropped to 2 million two years later.

Creation of the British Commonwealth. In 1931, the British government implemented the Statute of Westminster, which created the British Commonwealth of Nations, granted its members political equality, and freedom to reject any act passed by Parliament that related to a Dominion state.

6.1.3 *The Election of 1935*

MacDonald resigned his position in June 1935 because of ill health, and was succeeded by Stanley Baldwin, whose conservative coalition won 428 seats in new elections in November.

6.2 FRANCE

6.2.1 *France Under Andre Tardieu, 1929 – 1932*

On July 27, 1929, Poincare resigned as Premier because of

ill health. Over the next three years, the dominant figure in French politics was Andre Tardieu, who headed or played a role in Moderate cabinets.

Political and Social Reform. Tardieu tried to initiate political changes along American or British lines to create a stable two party system that would help France deal with the world economic crisis. He convinced the Laval government and the Chamber to accept electing its members by a plurality vote, though the Senate rejected it. In 1930, the government passed France's most important social welfare legislation, the National Workingmen's Insurance Law. It provided various forms of financial aid for illness, retirement, and death.

The Economy. The Depression did not hit France until late 1931, and it took it four years to begin to recover from it. At first, however, the country seemed immune to the Depression and the economy boomed. Its manufacturing indices reached a peak in 1929, but began gradually to slide through 1932. The economy recovered the following year, and dropped again through 1935.

6.2.2 *Return of the Cartel des Gauches, 1932 – 1934*

The defeat of the Moderates and the return of the leftists in the elections of May 1, 1932, reflected growing concern over the economy and failed efforts of the government to respond to the country's problems.

Political Problems and Reform. France remained plagued by differences over economic reform between the Radicals and the Socialists. The latter advocated nationalization of major factories, expanded social reforms, and public works programs for the unemployed, while the Radicals sought a reduction in government spending. This instability was also reflected in the fact that there were six Cabinets between June 1932 and February 1934.

Rise of Political Extremists. The government's inability to deal with the country's economic and political problems saw the emergence of a number of radical groups from across the political spectrum. Some of the more prominent were the Fascist *Francistes*, the *Solidarite Francaise*, the *"Cagoulards"* (Comite Secret d'Action Revoluntionnaire), the *Parti Populaire Francaise (PPF)* and the *Jeunesses Patriotes*. Not as radical, though still on the right were the *Croix de Feu* and the *Action Francaise*. At the other extreme was the French Communist Party.

The Stavisky Scandal. The growing influence of these groups exploded on February 6, 1934, around a scandal involving a con-man with government connections, Serge Stavisky. After his suicide on the eve of his arrest in December 1933, the scandal and his reported involvement with high government officials stimulated a growing crescendo of criticism that culminated in riots between rightist and leftist factions that resulted in 15 dead and 1,500 to 1,600 injured. The demonstrations and riots, viewed by some as a rightist effort to seize power, brought about the collapse of the Daladier government. He was immediately succeeded by ex-President Gaston Doumergue, who put together a coalition cabinet dominated by Moderates as well as Radicals and Rightists. It contained six former premiers and Marshal Petain.

6.2.3 Struggle for Stability, 1934 – 1935

The Government of Gaston Doumergue, 1934 – 1935. The accession of Doumergue (who had been President from 1924 to 1931) with his "National Union" cabinet, stabilized the public crisis, while the new Premier – influenced by Tardieu – used radio to try to convince the public of the need to increase the power of the President, Albert Lebrum (1932 – 1940), to enable the Premier to dissolve the legislature. Discontent with Doumergue's tactics resulted in resignations from his Cabinet and its fall in November 1934.

The Government of Pierre Laval, 1934 – 1935. Between November 1934 and June 1935, France had two more governments under Pierre-Etienne Flandin and F. Bouisson. The situation somewhat stabilized with the selection of Pierre Laval as Premier, who served from June 1935 through January 1936. Laval's controversial policies, strengthened by the ability to pass laws without legislative approval, were to deflate the economy, cut government expenditures, and remain on the gold standard. Laval's government fell in early 1936.

6.3   GERMANY

6.3.1   *The Young Plan*

One of the last accomplishments of Stresemann before his death on October 3 was the Young Plan, an altered reparations proposal that required Germany to make yearly payments for 59 years that varied from 1.6 to 2.4 billion Reichsmarks. In return, the Allies removed all foreign controls on Germany's economy and agreed to leave the Rhineland the following year. Efforts by the conservative extremists to stop Reichstag adoption of the Young Plan failed miserably, while a national referendum on the reactionary bill suffered the same fate.

6.3.2   *Germany and the Depression*

The Depression had a dramatic effect on the German economy and politics. German exports, which had peaked at 13.5 billion marks in 1929, fell to 12 billion marks in 1930, and to 5.7 billion marks two years later. Imports suffered the same fate, going from 14 billion marks in 1928 to 4.7 billion marks in 1932. The country's national income dropped 20% during this period, while unemployment rose from 1,320,000 in 1929 to 6 million by January 1932. This meant that 43% of the

German work force were without jobs (compared to one-quarter of the work force in the U.S.).

6.3.3   *The Rise of Adolf Hitler and Nazism.*

The history of Nazism is deeply intertwined with that of its leader, Adolf Hitler.

Hitler's Early Career to 1918. Adolf Hitler was born on April 20, 1889, in the Austrian village of Braunau-am-Inn, to a petty official. A frustrated artist, he moved to Vienna where he unsuccessfully tried to become a student in the Vienna Academy of Fine Arts. He then became an itinerant artist, living in hovels, until the advent of the World War, which he welcomed. His four years at the front were the most meaningful of his life up to that time, and he emerged a decorated corporal with a mission now to go into politics to restore his country's bruised honor.

Early Nazism. In 1919, Hitler joined the German Workers Party (DAP), which he soon took over and renamed the National Socialist German Workers Party (NAZI). In 1920, the Party adopted a 25-point program that included treaty revision, anti-Semitism, economic, and other social changes. They also created a defense cadre of the ***Sturmabteilung*** (SA), "Storm Troopers," or "brown shirts," which was to help the party seize power. Some of the more significant early Nazi leaders were Ernst Röhm, who helped build up the SA; Dietrich Eckart, first head of the Party paper, the ***Volkischer Beobachter;*** Alfred Rosenberg, who replaced Eckart as editor of ***Volkischer Beobachter*** and became the Party's chief ideologist; Hermann Göring, World War I flying ace, who took over the SA in 1922; and Rudolf Hess, who became Hitler's secretary.

The Beer Hall Putsch, 1923. In the midst of the country's severe economic crisis in 1923, the Party, which now had

55,000 members, tried to seize power, first by a march on Berlin, and then, when this seemed impossible, on Munich. The march was stopped by police, and Hitler and his supporters were arrested. Their trial, which Hitler used to voice Nazi ideals, gained him a national reputation. Though sentenced to five years imprisonment, he was released after eight months. While incarcerated, he dictated *Mein Kampf* to Rudolf Hess.

6.3.4 *The Nazi Movement, 1924 – 1929*

Hitler's failed *coup* and imprisonment convinced him to seek power through legitimate political channels, which would require transforming the Nazi Party. To do this, he reasserted singular control over the movement from 1924 to 1926. Party districts were set up throughout Germany, overseen by *Gaulieters* personally appointed by Hitler.

They were subdivided into *Kreise* (districts), and then *Ortsgruppen* (local chapters). A court system, the *Uschla*, oversaw the Party structure. The Party grew from 27,000 in 1925 to 108,000 in 1929. A number of new leaders emerged at this time, including Joseph Goebbels, who became Party Chief in Berlin and later Hitler's propaganda chief, and Heinrich Himmler, who became head of Hitler's private body guard, the SS (*Schutzstaffel*), in 1929.

6.3.5 *Weimar Politics, 1930 – 1933*

Germany's economic woes and the government's seeming inability to deal with them, underlined the weaknesses of the country's political system and provided the Nazis with new opportunities.

The Weimar Paralysis. In March 17, 1930, the alliance of Social Democratic, DVP and other parties collapsed over who should shoulder unemployment benefit costs. A new coalition, under Heinrich Breunig, tried to promote a policy of government economic retrenchment, and deflation, which the Reichstag rejected. Consequently, President Hindenburg invoked Article 48 of the Constitution, which enabled him to order the implementation of Breunig's program. The Reichstag overrode the decree, which forced the government's fall and new elections:

1) *Reichstag Elections of September 14, 1930.* The September 14 elections surprised everyone. The Nazis saw their 1928 vote jump from 800,000 to 6.5 million (18.3% of the vote), which gave them 107 Reichstag seats, second only to the Social Democrats, who fell from 152 to 143 seats. Bruenig, however, continued to serve as Chancellor of a weak coalition with the support of Hindenburg and rule by presidential decree. His policies failed to resolve the country's growing economic dilemmas.

2) *Presidential Elections of 1932.* Hindenburg's seven year presidential term expired in 1932, and he was convinced to run for reelection to stop Hitler from becoming President in the first ballot of March 13. Hitler got only 30% of the vote (11.3 million) to Hindenburg's 49.45% (18.6 million). Since German law required the new president to have a majority of the votes, a runoff was held on April 10 between Hindenburg, Hitler, and the Communist candidate, Thalmann. Hindenburg received 19.3 million votes (53%), Hitler 13.4 million (37%), and Thalmann 2.2 million votes.

The von Papen Chancellorship. On June 1, Bruenig was replaced by Franz von Papen, who formed a government made up of aristocratic conservatives and others that he and Hindenburg hoped would keep Hitler from power. He held new elections on July 31 that saw the Nazis win 230 Reichstag seats with 37% of the vote (13.7 million), and the Communists 89 seats. Offered the Vice Chancellorship and an opportunity to join a coalition government, Hitler refused. Von Papen, paralyzed politically, ruled by Presidential decree. Von Papen dissolved the Reichstag on September 12, and held new elections on November 6. The Nazis only got 30% of the vote and 196 Reichstag seats, while the Communists made substantial gains (120 seats from 89). Von Papen resigned in favor of Kurt von Schleicher, one of the President's closest advisers, as the new Chancellor.

6.3.6 *Hitler Becomes Chancellor*

Von Papen joined with Hitler to undermine Schleicher, and convinced Hindenburg to appoint Hitler as Chancellor and head of a new coalition cabinet with 3 seats for the Nazis.

Initial Efforts to Nazify Germany. Hitler dissolved the Reichstag and called for new elections on March 5. Using Presidential decree powers, he initiated a violent anti-communist campaign that included the lifting of certain press and civil freedoms. On February 27, the Reichstag burned which enabled Hitler to get Hindenburg to issue the "Ordinances for the Protection of the German State and Nation," that removed all civil and press liberties as part of a "revolution" against Communism. In the Reichstag elections of March 5, the Nazis only got 43.9% of the vote and 288 Reichstag seats but, through an alliance with the Nationalists, got majority control of the legislature.

The Enabling Act. Hitler now intensified his campaign against his political and other opponents, placing many of them in newly opened concentration camps. He also convinced Hindenburg to issue the Enabling Act on March 21 that allowed his Cabinet to pass laws and treaties without legislative backing for 4 years. The Reichstag gave him its full legal approval two days later, since many felt it was the only way legally to maintain some influence over his government.

Gleichschaltung. Once Hitler had full legislative power, he began a policy of *Gleichschaltung* (coordination) to bring all independent organizations and agencies throughout Germany under his control. All political parties were outlawed or forced to dissolve, and on July 14, 1933, the Nazi Party became the only legal party in Germany. In addition, German state authority was reduced and placed under Nazi-appointed *Stattholder* (governors), while the Party throughout Germany was divided into *Gaue* (Districts) under a Nazi-selected *Gauleiter*. In addition, non-Aryans and Nazi opponents were removed from the civil service, the court system, and higher education. On May 2, 1933, the government declared strikes illegal, abolished labor unions, and later forced all workers to join the German Labor Front (DAF) under Robert Ley. In 1934 the Reichsrat was abolished and a special People's Court was created to handle cases of treason. Finally, the secret police or GESTAPO (*Geheime Staatspolizei*) was created on April 24, 1933 under Göring to deal with opponents and operate concentration camps. The Party had its own security branch, the SD (*Sicherheitsdienst*) under Reinhard Heydrich.

6.3.7 Hitler Consolidates Power

The Röhm Purge ("The Night of the Long Knives"). A growing conflict over the direction of the Nazi "revolution" and the power of the SA *vis a vis* the SS and the German army had been brewing since Hitler took power. Ernst Röhm, head of the SA, wanted his forces to become the nucleus of a new German army headed by himself, while the military, Hitler, and the SS sought ways to contain his growing arrogance and independence. The solution was a violent purge on the night of June 30, 1934, coordinated by the GESTAPO and the SS, that resulted in the arrest and murder of Röhm plus 84 SA leaders,

85

as well as scores of other opponents that Hitler decided to eliminate under the cloud of his purge.

The Death of Hindenburg. The final barrier to Hitler's full consolidation of power in Germany was overcome with the death of Hindenburg on August 2, 1934. Hitler now combined the offices of President and Chancellor, and required all civil servants and workers to take a personal oath to him as the "Führer of the German Reich and people."

6.3.8   Religion and Anti-Semitism

Christian Groups. A state Protestant church of "German Christians" under a Bishop of the Reich, Ludwig Muller, was created in 1934. An underground opposition "Confessing Church" was formed under Martin Niemoller that suffered from severe persecution. On July 8, 1933, the government signed a Concordat with the Vatican that promised to allow traditional Catholic rights to continue in Germany. Unfortunately, the Nazis severely restricted Catholic religious practice, which created growing friction with the Vatican.

Jews. From the inception of the Nazi state in 1933, anti-Semitism was a constant theme and practice in all *Gleichschaltung* and nazification efforts. Illegal intimidation and harassment of Jews was coupled with rigid enforcement of civil service regulations that forbade employment of non-Aryans. This first wave of anti-Semitic activity culminated with the passage of the Nuremburg Laws of September 15, 1935, that deprived Jews of German citizenship and outlawed sexual or marital relations between Jews and other Germans, thus effectively isolating them from the mainstream of German society.

6.3.9   International Affairs

Hitler's international policies were closely linked to his rebuilding efforts to give him a strong economic and military base for an active, aggressive, independent foreign policy. On October 14, 1933, Hitler had his delegates walk out of the Disarmament Conference because he felt the Allied powers had reneged on an earlier promise to grant Germany arms equality. The Reich simultaneously quit the League of Nations. On January 26, 1934, Germany signed a non-aggression pact with Poland, which ended Germany's traditional anti-Polish foreign policy and broke France's encirclement of Germany via the Little Entente. This was followed by the Saarland's overwhelming decision to return to Germany. The culmination of Hitler's foreign policy moves, though, came with his March 15, 1935, announcement that Germany would no longer be bound by the military restrictions of the Treaty of Versailles, that it had already created an air force (*Luftwaffe*), and that the Reich would institute a draft to create an army of 500,000 men. Allied opposition to this move was compromised by England's decision to conclude a naval pact with Hitler on June 18, 1935, that restricted German naval tonnage (excluding submarines) to 35% of that for England.

6.4   ITALY

6.4.1   *Fascist Economic Reforms*

Increased economic well-being and growth were the promised results of Mussolini's restructuring of the economic system, while the general goals of the regime were to increase production through more efficient methods and land reclamation, with less dependency upon outside resources.

The Agricultural Sector. Efforts to increase the land under cultivation through reclamation projects were handicapped by Mussolini's emphasis on model propaganda projects, though the government had reclaimed 12 million acres by

1938. In fact, the small farmer suffered under these policies, because of Mussolini's quiet support of the larger landowner. In 1930, for example, 87.3% of the population controlled 13.2% of the land. The large farm owners, who made up only 0.5% of the population, controlled 41.9% of the land, while the mid-level farmer, who made up 12.2% of the population, controlled 44.9% of the countryside. Regardless, grain products did increase from 4,479 metric tons in 1924 to 8,184 metric tons in 1938, which enabled the government to cut grain imports by 75%. On the other hand, land needed to produce other agricultural products was used to increase wheat and grain output.

The Industrial Sector. To aid firms affected by the Depression, the government created the I.R.I. (*Instituto per la ricostruzione industriale*) which helped most big companies while smaller unsuccessful ones failed. The result was that the vast majority of Italy's major industry came under some form of government oversight. Italian production figures are unimpressive during this period, with increases for industrial production rising between 1928 and 1935. Steel output dropped, while pig-iron, oil products, and electrical output enjoyed moderate increases in the 1930's.

Overall Economic Development. The overall impact of Mussolini's economic programs saw the country's national income rise 15% from 1925 to 1935, with only a 10% per capita increase during this period. The value of exports dropped from 44,370 million lira in 1925 to 21,750 in 1938 because of the decision in 1927 to peg the lira to an artificially high exchange rate.

6.4.2 Church and State

The Lateran Accords. Until Mussolini's accession to power, the Pope had considered himself a prisoner in the Vatican. In 1926, Mussolini's government began talks to resolve this issue, which resulted in the Lateran Accords of February 11, 1929:

1) *The Treaty.* Italy recognized the Vatican as an independent state, with the Pope as its head, while the papacy recognized Italian independence.

2) *The Concordat.* Catholicism was made the official state religion of Italy, and religious teaching was required in all secondary schools. Church marriages were now fully legal, while the state could veto papal appointments of bishops. In addition, the clergy would declare loyalty to the Italian state.

3) *Financial Settlement.* The government agreed to pay the Church a financial settlement of 1.75 billion lira for the seizure of Church territory in 1860 – 1870.

State-Church Conflict. A conflict soon broke out over youth education and in May 1931 Mussolini dissolved the Catholic Action's youth groups. The Pope responded with an encyclical, *Non abbiamo bisogno*, which defended these groups, and criticized the Fascist deification of the state. Mussolini agreed later that year to allow Catholic Action to resume limited youth work.

6.4.3 *Foreign Policy*

The appointment of Adolph Hitler as Chancellor of Germany in early 1933 provided Mussolini with his most important thrust of diplomatic action since he came to power, while it underlined the currency of fascism as a ruling ideology and strengthened his claim to revision of the 1919 Paris Peace accords.

Four Power Pact (1933). Since the late 1920's, Mussolini began to support German claims for revision of the Treaty of Versailles to strengthen ties with that country and to counterbalance France, a nation he strongly disliked. These goals were current in his Four Power Pact proposal of March 1933 that envisioned a concert of powers – England, France, Italy, and Germany – that included arms parity for the Reich. French opposition to arms equality and treaty revision, plus concerns that the new consortium would replace the League of Nations, saw an extremely weakened agreement signed in June that was ultimately accepted only by Italy and Germany.

Rome Protocols (1934). In an effort to counter the significance of France's Little Entente with Czechoslovakia, Yugoslavia, and Rumania, Mussolini concluded the Rome Protocols with Austria and Hungary on March 17, 1934, that created a protective bond of friendship between the three countries.

Nazi Coup Attempt in Austria (1934). The first test of the new alliance between Italy and Austria came in July 1934, when German-directed Nazis tried to seize control of the Austrian government. Mussolini, opposed to any German *Anschluss* with Austria, mobilized Italian forces along the northern Renner Pass as a warning to Hitler. The *coup* collapsed from lack of direct German aid.

Stresa Front (1935). In response to Hitler's announcement of German rearmament in violation of the Treaty of Versailles on March 16, 1935, France, England, and Italy met at Stresa in northern Italy on April 11 – 14, and concluded agreements that pledged joint military collaboration if Germany moved against Austria or along the Rhine. The three states criticized Germany's recent decision to remilitarize and appealed to the Council of the League of Nations on the matter.

The Ethiopian Crisis. Ethiopia (Abyssinia) became an area of strong Italian interest in the 1880's. The coastal region was slowly brought under Italian control until the Italian defeat at Ethiopian hands at Adowa in 1894. In 1906, the country's autonomy was recognized and in 1923 it joined the League of Nations.

Mussolini's Designs. Mussolini, driven by a strong patriotic desire to avenge the humiliation at Adowa and to create an empire to thwart domestic concerns over the country's economic problems, searched for the proper moment to seize the country. Acquisition of Ethiopia would enable him to join Italy's two colonies of Eritrea and Somalia, which could become a new area of Italian colonization.

Wal Wal Incident. Mussolini, who had been preparing for war with Ethiopia since 1932, established a military base at Wal Wal in Ethiopian territory. Beginning in December 1934, a series of minor conflicts took place between the two countries, which gave Mussolini an excuse to plan for the full takeover of the country in the near future.

Invasion of Ethiopia (1935). Mussolini, who refused to accept arbitration over Ethiopia, used Europe's growing concern over Hitler's moves there to cover his own secret designs in Ethiopia. On October 2, 1935, Italy invaded Ethiopia, while the League of Nations, which had received four appeals from Ethiopia since January about Italian territorial transgressions, finally voted to adopt economic sanctions against Mussolini. Unfortunately, the League failed to stop shipments of oil to Italy and continued to allow it to use the Suez Canal. On May 9, 1936, Italy formally annexed the country and joined it to Somalia and Eritrea, which now became known as Italian East Africa.

6.5   SOVIET RUSSIA

The period from 1929 to 1935 was a time of tremendous upheaval for the USSR as Stalin tried to initiate major programs of collectivization of agriculture and massive industrial development.

6.5.1   *Collectivization of Soviet Agriculture*

At the end of 1927, Stalin, concerned over problems of grain supply, ordered the gradual consolidation of the country's 25 million small farms, on which 80% of the population lived, into state-run collective farms.

Agriculture in the First Five Year Plan (1928 – 1932). According to the Plan's goals, agricultural output was to rise 150% over five years, and 20% of the country's private farms transformed into collectives.

War Against the Kulaks. In an effort to link agricultural efficiency with heavy industrial development, Stalin decided by the end of 1929 to rapidly collectivize the country's entire agriculture system. Because of earlier resistance from peasants between 1927 and 1929, Stalin ordered war against the kulak or "middle class" peasant class. Some sources claim that as many as 5 million ill-defined kulaks were internally deported during this period.

Peasant Resistance. The above, combined with forced grain seizures, triggered massive, bloody resistance in the country-side. Though half of the nation's peasants were forced onto collectives during this period, they destroyed a great deal of Russia's livestock in the process. In the spring of 1930, Stalin called a momentary halt to the process, which prompted many peasants to leave the state farms.

The State Farm System. Over the next seven years, the entire Soviet system was collectivized, and all peasants forced onto state farms. The major types of farms were the Sovkhoz, which were initially preferred by the government until 1935, where peasants were paid for their labor; and the *Kovkhoz*, or collective farm, where the peasants gave the government a percentage of their crops and kept the surplus. The three types of *Kovkhozs* were the *Artel*, the most common, where the peasant had a small garden plot; the *Toz*, where he owned his tools and animals; and the *Commune*, where the state owned everything. One of the most important components of the collective and the state farm system was the Machine Tractor Station (MTS) which controlled the tractors and farm equipment for various government run farms.

Results of Collectivization. Direct and indirect deaths from Stalin's collectivization efforts totaled 14.5 million. Grain production levels did not reach 1928 levels until 1935. It did, though, break the back of rural peasant independence and created a totalitarian network of control throughout the countryside. It also undercut his own base of political support within the Party.

6.5.2 Industrialization

Stalin, concerned that Russia would fall irreparably behind the West industrially, hoped to achieve industrial parity with the West in a decade. At this time, Russia was barely on par with Italy in pig-iron and steel production. To stimulate workers, labor unions lost their autonomy and workers, including impressed peasants, were forced to work at locations and under conditions determined by the state. A special "Turnover" tax was placed on all goods throughout the country to help pay for industrialization.

Industrialization and the First Five Year Plan (1928 – 1932). The industrialization goals of the First Five Year Plan, supported hopefully by a flourishing agricultural system, were to increase total industrial production by 236%, heavy industry by 330%, coal, 200%, electrical output, 400%, and pig-iron production, 300%. Workers were to increase their efforts over 100%. Efficiency was also a hallmark of this program, and production costs were to drop by over a third, and prices by a quarter.

In most instances, the Plan's unrealistic goals were hard to meet. Regardless, steel production doubled, though it fell short of the Plan's goals, as did oil and hard coal output. Total industrial production, however, did barely surpass the Plan's expectations.

Second Five Year Plan (1933 – 1937). The Second Five Year Plan was adopted by the XVII Party Congress in early 1934. Its economic and production targets were less severe than the first Plan, and thus more was achieved. The model for workers was Alexis Stakhanov, a coal miner who met 1400% of his quota in the fall of 1935. A Stakhanovite movement arose to stimulate workers to greater efforts. By the end of the Second Plan, Soviet Russia had emerged as a leading world industrial power, though at great costs. It gave up quality for quantity, and created tremendous social and economic discord that still affects the USSR. The tactics used by Stalin to institute his economic reforms formed the nucleus of his totalitarian system, while reaction to them within the Party led to the Purges.

6.5.3 *Party Politics and the Origin of the Purges*

The tremendous upheaval caused by forced collectivization, blended with the remnants of the Rightist conflict with Stalin, prompted the Soviet leader to initiate one of the country's periodic purges of the Party. Approved by the top leadership, suspected opponents were driven from Party ranks

94

while Zinoviev and Kamenev were briefly exiled to Siberia. Continued uncertainty over the best policies to follow after the initiation of the Second Five Year Plan ended with the murder at the end of 1934 of Sergei Kirov, Stalin's supposed heir, and Leningrad party chief. Though the reasons for Kirov's murder are still unclear, his more liberal tendencies, plus his growing popularity, made him a threat to the Soviet leader. In the spring of 1935, the recently renamed and organized secret police, the NKVD, oversaw the beginnings of a new, violent Purge that eradicated 70% of the 1934 Central Committee, and a large percentage of the upper military ranks. Stalin sent between 8 and 9 million to camps and prisons, and caused untold deaths before the Purges ended in 1938.

6.5.4   *Foreign Policy, 1929 – 1935*

The period from 1929 to 1933 saw the USSR retreat inward as the bulk of its energies were put into domestic economic growth. Regardless, Stalin remained sensitive to growing aggression and ideological threats abroad such as the Japanese invasion of Manchuria in 1931 and Hitler's appointment as Chancellor. As a result, Russia left its cocoon in 1934, joined the League of Nations, and became an advocate of "collective security" while the Comintern adopted Popular Front tactics, allying with other parties against fascism, to strengthen the USSR's international posture. Diplomatically, in addition to League membership, the Soviet Union completed a military pact with France.

CHAPTER 7

INTERNATIONAL DEVELOPMENTS, 1918 – 1935

7.1 THE LEAGUE OF NATIONS

Efforts to create some international body to arbitrate international conflicts gained credence with the creation of a Permanent Court of International Justice to handle such matters at the First Hague Conference (1899). At a similar meeting eight years later, concern was expressed over Europe's growing arms race, though no country was willing to give the Permanent Court adequate authority to serve as a legitimate arbitrator. Leon Bourgeois, a French statesman, however, pushed for some sort of strong international peacekeeping body, but no major efforts towards this goal were initiated until 1915, when pro-League of Nations organizations arose in the United States and Great Britain. Support for such a body grew as the war lengthened, and creation of such an organization became the cornerstone of President Woodrow Wilson's post-war policy, enunciated in his "Fourteen Points" speech before Congress on January 8, 1918. His last point called for an international chamber of states to guarantee national autonomy and independence.

At the Paris Peace Conference, the major Allied leaders created a Commission for the League to draft its constitution, while the covenant of the League was placed in the Treaty of Versailles.

7.1.1 *The Preamble of the League's Covenant*

This statement defined the League's purposes, which were to work for international friendship, peace, and security. To attain this, its members agreed to avoid war, maintain peaceful relations with other countries, and honor international law and accords.

7.1.2 *The Organization of the League of Nations*

Headquartered in Geneva, the League came into existence as the result of an Allied resolution announcing their intentions on January 25, 1919, and the signing of the Treaty of Versailles on June 28, 1919.

The Covenant. The 26 article Covenant determined terms of membership and withdrawal (two-thirds vote to join and two years notice to resign) and means to amend the Covenant (unanimous vote of Council with majority approval from Assembly).

The Council. The League's Council originally consisted of five permanent members (France, Italy, England, Japan, and the U.S.), though the U.S. seat was left vacant because the U.S. Senate refused to ratify the Treaty of Versailles. Germany filled the vacancy in 1926. It also had four 1-year rotating seats (increased to 6 in 1922, and raised to 9 seats in 1926). The Council, with each member having one vote, could discuss any matter that threatened international stability, and could recommend action to member states. It also had the right, according to Article 8 of the League Covenant, to seek ways to reduce arms strength, while Articles 10 through 17 gave it the authority to search for means to stop war. It could recommend through a unanimous vote ways to stop aggression, and could suggest economic sanctions and other tactics to enforce its decisions, though its military ability to enforce its decisions was vague. It met four times a year from 1923 to 1929, and then three times annually afterwards.

The Assembly. The League's legislative body had similar debating and discussion authority, though it had no legislative powers. It initially had 43 members, which rose to 49 by the mid-1930's, though six others, including Italy, Germany, and Japan, withdrew their membership during the same period. The USSR, which joined in 1934, was expelled six years later.

The Permanent Court of International Justice (World Court). The League's judicial responsibilities were handled by the "World Court" that was located at The Hague in The Netherlands. Created in 1921 and opened the following year, it would consider and advise on any case from any nation or the League, acting as an arbiter to prevent international conflict. The court's decisions were not binding: it relied on voluntary submission to its decisions. It initially had eleven judges (later 15) selected for five year terms by the League.

The Secretariat. The day-to-day affairs of the League were administered by the General Secretary (Sir Eric Drummond to 1933; J. Avenol afterwards) and his bureaucracy, the Secretariat, which was composed of an international collection of League civil servants.

Other League Organizations. Lesser known functions of the League dealt with the efforts of its International Labor Organization (I.L.O.) which tried to find ways to reduce labor-management and class tensions; and the Mandates Commission, which oversaw territories taken from the Central Powers and were administered – as a prelude to independence – under mandate from League members. In addition, the League tried to provide medical, economic, and social welfare aid to depressed parts of the world.

7.2   THE WASHINGTON CONFERENCE, 1921 – 1922

The first post-war effort to deal with problems of disarmament was the Washington Conference (November 1921 – February 1922). Its participants, which included the major powers in Europe and Asia plus the meeting's sponsor, the United States, discussed a number of problems that resulted in three separate agreements:

7.2.1   *The Washington Naval Treaty (Five Power Treaty)*

France, Italy, England, the United States, and Japan agreed to halt battleship construction for ten years, while limiting or reducing capital shipping levels to 525,000 tons for the U.S. and England, 315,000 tons for Japan, and 175,000 tons for Italy and France.

7.2.2   *The Four Power Treaty*

The United States, England, France, and Japan agreed not to seek further Pacific expansion or increased naval strength there and to respect the Pacific holdings of the other signatory powers.

7.2.3   *The Nine Power Treaty*

To grant China some sense of autonomy not offered at the Paris Peace Conference, an agreement signed by Japan, the

Netherlands, Portugal, Belgium, Italy, France, England, the U.S., and China, after Japan's agreement to return Kiachow to China, guaranteed China's independence and territorial autonomy.

7.3   THE DRAFT TREATY OF MUTUAL ASSISTANCE (1923)

In the ongoing search for ways to encourage continuing disarmament talks and provide security, particularly for France, which continued to worry about future threats from Germany, the League of Nations had set up a Temporary Mixed Commission (TMC) of specialists to study disarmament. In an effort to find a technical-political solution to protect nations that did reduce arms, the TMC submitted a Draft Treaty of Mutual Assistance to the League Assembly in September 1923, that would enable the Council to determine, after a war broke out, the guilty nation, and to intervene on the side of the victim. Approved by the Assembly, and submitted to all countries, France, Italy, and Japan were the only major states to support it. All other important countries rejected it because they were concerned about its regional limitations, its protection for only those that disarmed, and the League's role in such actions, particularly in defining aggression.

7.4   THE GENEVA PROTOCOL (1924)

The failure of many important nations to accept the Draft Treaty prompted the British and the French to search for a different solution to the problem of protection for those that disarmed that would quell some of the fears that sank the Draft Treaty. The result was the Protocol for the Pacific Settlement of International Disputes, or the Geneva Protocol, that stated that the nation that refused to submit to arbitration by the

World Court, the League Council, or special arbitrators, would be termed the aggressor. The agreement was tied to a further disarmament conference and a network of regional security pacts. Approved by the Assembly in October 1924, France and its Little Entente allies backed it quickly. England, however, backed by Commonwealth members, disapproved because of the broad commitments involved, which sank any prospect of final approval of the Protocol.

7.5   THE LOCARNO PACT (1925)

Failure of the European powers to create some type of international system to prevent aggression was followed by regional efforts, prompted by Germany's visionary Foreign Minister, Gustav Stresemann, who in early 1925 approached England and France about an accord whereby Germany would accept its western borders in return for early Allied withdrawal from the demilitarized Rhine area. Stresemann also wanted League membership for his country. While England responded with guarded regional interest, France hesitated. Six months later, after consultation with its eastern allies, Paris countered with a proposal that would include similar provisions for Germany's eastern borders, secured by a mutual assistance pact between Italy, Great Britain, and France. These countries, along with Belgium, Czechoslovakia, and Poland, met for two months in Locarno, Switzerland, and concluded a number of separate agreements.

7.5.1   *Treaty of Mutual Guarantees (Rhineland Pact)*

Signed on October 16, 1925, by England, France, Italy, Germany and Belgium, they guaranteed Germany's western boundaries and accepted the Versailles settlement's demilitarized zones. Italy and Great Britain agreed militarily to defend these lines if flagrantly violated.

7.5.2   Arbitration Settlements

In the same spirit, Germany signed arbitration dispute accords that mirrored the Geneva Protocol with France, Belgium, Poland, and Czechoslovakia, and required acceptance of League-determined settlements.

7.5.3   Eastern Accords

Since Germany would only agree to arbitration and not finalize its eastern border, France separately signed guarantees with Poland and Czechoslovakia to defend their frontiers.

7.5.4   Germany Joins the League

The Locarno Pact would go into force when Germany joined the League, which it did on September 10, 1926, acquiring, after some dispute, the U.S.'s permanent seat on the Council. France and Belgium began to withdraw from the Rhineland, though they left a token force there until 1930.

7.6   THE PACT OF PARIS (KELLOGG-BRIAND PACT)

The Locarno Pact heralded a new period in European relations known as the "Era of Locarno" that marked the end of post-war conflict and the beginning of a more normal period of diplomatic friendship and cooperation. It reached its peak, idealistically, with the Franco-American effort in 1928 to seek an international statement to outlaw war. The seed for this new proposal arose on the eve of the tenth anniversary of the American entrance into the World War, and centered around interest in a mutual statement outlawing war as a theme in national policy. In December 1927, Frank Kellogg, the American Secretary of State, proposed that this policy be offered to all nations in the form of a treaty. On August 27, 1928, fifteen countries, including the U.S., Germany, France, Italy and Japan, signed this accord with some minor limitations, which renounced war as a means of solving differences and as a tool of national policy. Within five years, 50 other countries signed the agreement. Unfortunately, without something more than idealism to back it up, the Kellogg-Briand Pact had little practical meaning.

7.7 THE WANING SEARCH FOR DISARMAMENT

The Depression did not diminish the desire for disarmament, but it did add a new series of problems and concerns that made the search more difficult, and, with growing threats of aggression in Asia and Europe, destroyed these efforts.

7.7.1 *London Naval Disarmament Treaty*

In March 1930, Great Britain and the United States sought to expand the naval limitation terms of the Five Power Treaty of 1922. France and Italy could not agree on terms, while the U.S., England, and Japan accepted mild reductions in cruiser and destroyer strength.

7.7.2 *World Disarmament Conference*

The starting point for implementation of the 1924 Geneva Protocol was a disarmament conference, which, though envisioned for 1925, did not convene until February 5, 1932. Attended by 60 countries including the USSR and the United States, initial discussions centered around a French proposal that wanted a protective monitoring system and required arbitration before considering disarmament. On the other hand, the U.S. asked for one-third reduction of current treaty shipping strength. Germany countered with demands for arms parity before disarmament. Though this was a front for more complex issues, the Germans left the conference when rebuffed in September 1932, only to be lured back later by a Five Power statement that agreed, in spirit, to Germany's demand. Hitler's accession to power on January 30, 1933, halted any further consideration of this point, which prompted Germany's withdrawal from the conference and the League. This, and France's continued insistence on pre-disarmament security guarantees, neutralized conference efforts, and it closed in failure in June 1934.

7.8   LEAGUE AND ALLIED RESPONSE TO AGGRESSION

By 1931, international attention increasingly turned to growing acts or threats of aggression in Europe and Asia, and transformed Europe from a world that hoped for eternal peace to a Continent searching desperately for ways to contain growing aggression.

7.8.1   *The League's Lytton Report and Manchuria*

On September 19, 1931, the Japanese Kwantung Army, acting independently of the government in Tokyo, began the gradual conquest of Manchuria after fabricating an incident at Mukden to justify their actions. Ultimately, they created a puppet state, Manchukuo, under the last Chinese emperor, Henry Pu Yi. China's League protest resulted in the creation of an investigatory commission under the Earl of Lytton, that criticized Japan's actions and recommended a negotiated settlement that would have allowed Japan to retain most of its conquest. Japan responded by resigning from the League on January 24, 1933.

7.8.2 *The Stresa Front*

Hitler's announcement on March 15, 1935, of Germany's decisions to rearm and to introduce conscription in violation of the Treaty of Versailles prompted the leaders of England, France, and Italy to meet in Stresa, Italy (April 11 – 14) to discuss a response. They condemned Germany's actions, underlined their commitment to the Locarno Pact, and reaffirmed the support they collectively gave for Austria's independence in early 1934. Prompted by these actions, the League Council also rebuked Germany, and created an investigatory committee to search for economic means to punish the Reich. Great Britain's decision, however, to protect separately its naval strength *vis a vis* a German buildup in the Anglo-German Naval Treaty of June 18, 1935, effectively compromised the significance of the Stresa Front.

7.8.3 *Italy and Ethiopia*

By the end of 1934, Italy had begun to create a number of incidents in Ethiopia as a prelude to complete absorption of that country. The Emperor of Ethiopia, Haile Sellasie, appealed directly to the League on the matter in January 1935. Franco-British efforts to mediate the crisis failed, while Ethiopia continued to look to the League to contain Italian aggression. Reluctance to do more than voice verbal objections to Italian actions because of fear, particularly on the part of the French, that Italy would draw closer to Germany, convinced Mussolini that he could act with impunity. Consequently, on October 3, 1935, Italy invaded Ethiopia, which prompted the League to declare the former country the aggressor. Ineffective economic sanctions followed on October 19. Independent Anglo-French efforts to halt separately Italian aggression by granting Mussolini most of Ethiopia (with economic predominance) failed in December because of a strong public outcry over the terms. Italy completed its conquest in early May 1935, and annexed Ethiopia on May 9.

ITALIAN POSSESSIONS TO 1940

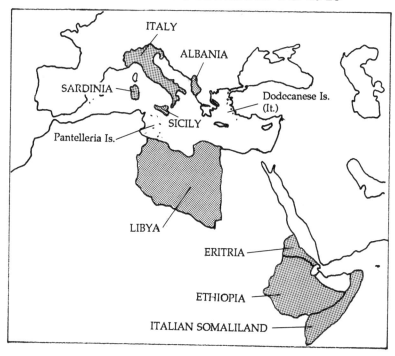

"The ESSENTIALS" of Math & Science

Each book in the ESSENTIALS series offers all essential information of the field it covers. It summarizes what every textbook in the particular field must include, and is designed to help students in preparing for exams and doing homework. The ESSENTIALS are excellent supplements to any class text.

The ESSENTIALS are complete, concise, with quick access to needed information, and provide a handy reference source at all times. The ESSENTIALS are prepared with REA's customary concern for high professional quality and student needs.

Available in the following titles:

Advanced Calculus I & II
Algebra & Trigonometry I & II
Anthropology
Automatic Control Systems /
   Robotics I & II
Biology I & II
Boolean Algebra
Calculus I, II & III
Chemistry
Complex Variables I & II
Differential Equations I & II
Electric Circuits I & II
Electromagnetics I & II

Electronic Communications I & II
Electronics I & II
Finite & Discrete Math
Fluid Mechanics /
   Dynamics I & II
Fourier Analysis
Geometry I & II
Group Theory I & II
Heat Transfer I & II
LaPlace Transforms
Linear Algebra
Math for Engineers I & II
Mechanics I, II & III

Modern Algebra
Numerical Analysis I & II
Organic Chemistry I & II
Physical Chemistry I & II
Physics I & II
Set Theory
Statistics I & II
Strength of Materials &
   Mechanics of Solids I & II
Thermodynamics I & II
Topology
Transport Phenomena I & II
Vector Analysis

If you would like more information about any of these books,
complete the coupon below and return it to us or go to your local bookstore.

RESEARCH & EDUCATION ASSOCIATION
61 Ethel Road W. • Piscataway, New Jersey 08854
Phone: (908) 819-8880

Please send me more information about your Essentials Books

Name _____

Address _____

City _____ State _____ Zip _____

Available at your local bookstore or order directly from us by sending in coupon below.

"The ESSENTIALS" of
ACCOUNTING & BUSINESS

Each book in the Accounting and Business ESSENTIALS series offers all essential information about the subject it covers. It includes every important principle and concept, and is designed to help students in preparing for exams and doing homework. The Accounting and Business ESSENTIALS are excellent supplements to any class text or course of study.

The Accounting and Business ESSENTIALS are complete and concise, with quick access to needed information. They also provide a handy reference source at all times. The Accounting and Business ESSENTIALS are prepared with REA's customary concern for high professional quality and student needs.

Available titles include:

Accounting I & II	Financial Management
Advanced Accounting I & II	Income Taxation
Advertising	Intermediate Accounting I & II
Auditing	Microeconomics
Business Law I & II	Macroeconomics I & II
Business Statistics I & II	Marketing Principles
Corporate Taxation	Money & Banking I & II
Cost & Managerial Accounting I & II	

If you would like more information about any of these books,
complete the coupon below and return it to us or go to your local bookstore.

"The ESSENTIALS" of HISTORY

REA's **Essentials of History** series offers a new approach to the study of history that is different from what has been available previously. Compared with conventional history outlines, the **Essentials of History** offer far more detail, with fuller explanations and interpretations of historical events and developments. Compared with voluminous historical tomes and textbooks, the **Essentials of History** offer a far more concise, less ponderous overview of each of the periods they cover.

The **Essentials of History** provide quick access to needed information, and will serve as a handy reference source at all times. The **Essentials of History** are prepared with REA's customary concern for high professional quality and student needs.

UNITED STATES HISTORY

1500 to 1789 From Colony to Republic
1789 to 1841 The Developing Nation
1841 to 1877 Westward Expansion & the Civil War
1877 to 1912 Industrialism, Foreign Expansion & the Progressive Era
1912 to 1941 World War I, the Depression & the New Deal
America since 1941: Emergence as a World Power

EUROPEAN HISTORY

1450 to 1648 The Renaissance, Reformation & Wars of Religion

1648 to 1789 Bourbon, Baroque & the Enlightenment
1789 to 1848 Revolution & the New European Order
1848 to 1914 Realism & Materialism
1914 to 1935 World War I & Europe in Crisis
Europe since 1935: From World War II to the Demise of Communism

WORLD HISTORY

Ancient History (4,500BC to 500AD)
The Emergence of Western Civilization
Medieval History (500 to 1450AD)
The Middle Ages

*If you would like more information about any of these books,
complete the coupon below and return it to us or go to your local bookstore.*

REA's Test Preps
The Best in Test Preparations

The REA "Test Preps" are far more comprehensive than any other test series. They contain more tests with much more extensive explanations than others on the market. Each book provides several complete practice exams, based on the most recent tests given in the particular field. Every type of question likely to be given on the exams is included. Each individual test is followed by a complete answer key. **The answers are accompanied by full and detailed explanations.** By studying each test and the pertinent explanations, students will become well-prepared for the actual exam.

REA has published 40 Test Preparation volumes in several series. They include:

Advanced Placement Exams (APs)
Biology
Calculus AB & Calculus BC
Chemistry
Computer Science
English Literature & Composition
European History
Government & Politics
Physics
Psychology
United States History

College Board Achievement Tests (CBATs)
American History
Biology
Chemistry
English Composition

French
German
Literature
Mathematics Level I, II & IIC
Physics
Spanish

Graduate Record Exams (GREs)
Biology
Chemistry
Computer Science
Economics
Engineering
General
History
Literature in English
Mathematics
Physics
Political Science
Psychology

CBEST - California Basic Educational Skills Test
CDL - Commercial Drivers License Exam
ExCET - Exam for Certification of Educators in Texas
FE (EIT) - Fundamentals of Engineering Exam
GED - High School Equivalency Diploma Exam
GMAT - Graduate Management Admission Test
LSAT - Law School Admission Test
MCAT - Medical College Admission Test
NTE - National Teachers Exam
SAT - Scholastic Aptitude Test
TOEFL - Test of English as a Foreign Language

RESEARCH & EDUCATION ASSOCIATION
61 Ethel Road W. • Piscataway, New Jersey 08854
Phone: (908) 819-8880

Please send me more information about your Test Prep Books

Name _____

Address _____

City _____ State _____ Zip _____